THE GREATEST STORIES EVER TOLD

THE GREATEST STORIES EVER TOLD

Sampurna Chattarji

PUFFIN BOOKS

For Swayambhu, Sitara, Niall and Roshan

PUFFIN
Published by the Penguin Group
Penguin Books India Pvt Ltd, 11 Community Centre, Panchsheel Park, New Delhi
110 017, India
Penguin Group (USA) Inc., 375 Hudson Street, New York, New York 10014, USA
Penguin Group (Canada), 10 Alcorn Avenue, Toronto, Ontario, Canada M4V 3B2
(a division of Pearson Penguin Canada Inc.)
Penguin Books Ltd, 80 Strand, London WC2R 0RL, England
Penguin Ireland, 25 St Stephen's Green, Dublin 2, Ireland (a division of Penguin
Books Ltd)
Penguin Group (Australia), 250 Camberwell Road, Camberwell, Victoria 3124,
Australia (a division of Pearson Australia Group Pty Ltd)
Penguin Group (NZ), cnr Airborne and Rosedale Roads, Albany, Auckland 1310,
New Zealand (a division of Pearson New Zealand Ltd)
Penguin Group (South Africa) (Pty) Ltd, 24 Sturdee Avenue, Rosebank,
Johannesburg 2196, South Africa

Penguin Books Ltd, Registered Offices: 80 Strand, London WC2R 0RL, England

First published in Puffin by Penguin Books India 2004

Copyright © Sampurna Chattarji 2004

10 9 8 7 6 5 4 3 2 1

Typeset in AGaramond by Eleven Arts, Delhi-35

Printed at International Print-O-Pac, New Delhi

CONTENTS

Creation and the Fall 1

The End of the World 31

The Divine Child and the Evil King 57

The Prince Who Gave Up the Earth 85

The Tempter and the Holy Man 117

The Revelation 139

The Trial of Faith 173

The Flight of the Persecuted 201

The Miracle Worker 235

The Heroic Child 259

The Parable 295

The Godly Animal 321

Author's Note 351

About the Author 354

Guest of Reality

The Eternal Smile 107

The Marriage Feast 57

The Executioner 85

The Basement and the Holy Man 119

The Dwarf 149

Barabbas 174

The Sibyl 201

The Death of Ahasuerus 233

Pilgrim at Sea 259

The Holy Land 282

Herod and Mariamne 304

Guest of Reality 451

CREATION
& THE FALL

The brightness
was too
strong.

In the beginning was the light. The light was called Ahura Mazda. He was the Wise Lord, the Lord of Truth and Wisdom, Love and Life. He knew everything, even things that would happen after thousands and thousands of years. He also knew He had an enemy—darkness.

The darkness was called Angra Mainyu or the Demon of the Lie, and he had no idea that there was such a thing as light. So for three thousand years, he lay in some bottomless abyss, thinking the whole world was his.

Ahura Mazda, on the other hand, had used those three thousand years to do something more constructive than just lying about. Out of His own thoughts, He had begun to create the world. His thoughts took the shape of perfectly spiritual beings. Ahura Mazda was waiting for the time when He would give those perfectly spiritual beings bodies and movement and minds. He was also waiting for what He knew would happen any moment now.

A confrontation.

It happened just as He had foreseen. One day, Angra Mainyu, the Demon of the Lie, got up from his three-thousand-year long sleep, stretched himself and decided to see how the world had been getting on without him. It was the first time that he was going to leave the comfort of his home, where darkness hung like a thick curtain. As he climbed up and up, he saw a curious thing. What was that tear in the curtain? Some strange milky thing seemed to be pouring through the tear and hurting his eyes the closer he climbed. The closer he climbed, the larger the gap in the pitch-black curtain became. What had first seemed like a milky liquid was now like a torrent of sharp and glittering pain. He began to feel annoyed. What was this thing that hurt him so, and that he had no name for? He would climb out and put an end to it, that was for sure.

He reached the top. The sharp and glittering thing hit him with all the force of its brightness. He staggered. 'What is it?' he thought. Out of the centre of that brightness came the answer. 'So, this is called light,' Angra Mainyu thought. 'Well, *this* is the end of light!' And he rushed up to swallow the brightness and finish it off in one enormous gulp.

But the brightness was too strong.

Angra Mainyu and Ahura Mazda struggled with each other on the edge of that bottomless abyss. Even before Angra Mainyu realized what was happening he found himself falling, falling down down down till the light was only a memory in his dark mind. But how that memory tormented him! It was sharp, it was cruel, and it was stronger than him. There was only one way he could stop it. He would create fiends, fearsome creatures whose bodies would be made out of the sooty darkness, and whose minds would be bottomless voids of evil. With that army of dark fiends he would rise from the abyss again and snuff out the light forever.

It didn't take him long to carry out his plan. He felt a whole lot braver the second time he rose from his pit. The dark hosts were with him, a cluster of shadows impossible to distinguish one from the other, sinister heaving shapes whose breath was as cold as fear. The light would shrink back from this dark tide, he thought. And then he, Angra Mainyu, Demon of the Lie, would rule the world! Thinking such thoughts he burst out to face Ahura Mazda.

'Fight us if you dare,' he challenged the Lord of Light.

'But I do not wish to fight,' replied Ahura Mazda. 'I wish to make peace.'

'Aha,' gloated Angra Mainyu. 'He is afraid! He talks of peace out of fear! He takes one look at my army of demons and he faints!'

Aloud he said, 'I have no taste for peace. If you are as strong as you imagine, let the fight begin, so I can put an end to your imaginings. Once this battle is through, not one of your creations will remain!'

Ahura Mazda knew very well that no matter how hard and how long Angra Mainyu fought, he would never be able to overcome the forces of light. But He also knew that it was hopeless trying to make him understand that. Whatever He said or did, Angra Mainyu would fight. He would fight and he would lose. The sad part was that he would do all of this convinced of his own rightness, in a haze of ignorance and pride.

'Well then, let there be conflict,' Ahura Mazda said. 'But remember this, Angra Mainyu, you will not win. Not one of my creatures will be hurt. Yours, on the other hand, will all be destroyed. After nine thousand years you will find yourself ground into dust!'

Nine thousand years of conflict seemed like a good bargain to the ignorant Angra Mainyu. He did not believe a word Ahura Mazda said. For Angra Mainyu the truth was false, and the lie was truth. That is how he lived in his deep upside-down world of darkness, and that is where he now retreated to prepare new forces of evil.

Ahura Mazda was free to do His own work.

The first thing He created was the Good Mind and the Sky. Down in the pit, the first thing Angra Mainyu created was the Evil Mind and the Lie. It was a battle of wills. For every good thing Ahura Mazda created, its wicked opposite sprang up in the hidden regions of horror. Ahura Mazda knew and saw it all, but went on, unperturbed.

He summoned up an army of constellations out of the sky— the Great Bear, the Crab, the Hunter, the Scorpion and the Fish. Each constellation had a troop of small stars, commanded by four chieftains in the north, the south, the east and the west. They all bowed down to their kings—the moon and the sun. Happy with the way the newly-created sky twinkled and sparkled, Ahura Mazda turned His gaze away and made water and earth. Plants sprang up from the earth—the myrtle and the date, the wheat stalk and the barley grain. Animals began grazing and hunting on the wide plains and dense forests—the white goat, the black sheep, the two-humped camel, the yellow-kneed ox. And then at last, Ahura Mazda made man.

Unlike Ahura Mazda, Angra Mainyu, the Demon of the Lie, decided to give himself a little rest after completing his first day's work. Nine thousand years was a long time! A little nap would not come in the way of his dark plans to destroy the world. But when he woke from that little nap, he found that three thousand years had already passed! That didn't bother Angra Mainyu too much. What bothered him was that he had been woken up by a female demon with a most piercing voice.

'Awake!' she shrieked in his ear. 'Set me loose into the world of Ahura Mazda and his archangels! I cannot wait to poison the world he has made!'

Angra Mainyu's irritation vanished. Here was a demon after his heart! He kissed her on the forehead and granted her a wish.

'A man! A man!' she shrieked.

And because Angra Mainyu was so pleased with her he changed his own shape from that of a giant log-like lizard into a charming fifteen-year-old youth.

Filled with new zeal, Angra Mainyu leapt out of his hiding place to wreak havoc on Ahura Mazda's creations. He hurled himself like a malignant snake into the sky. He picked up the moving planets as if they were stones and flung them at the constellations. The constellations scattered. He hurtled down to the earth and dried up all the water in all the seas and rivers and lakes. He took one look at the fertile, flowering earth and filled it with poisonous scorpions and snakes and frogs and lizards. The earth shook with anger and despair, and great mountains rose up, groaning. He dried up all the plants with his hot breath. But the Angel of Vegetation mixed the dried-up remains with the tears of the Angel of Rain, and new plants sprang up all over the earth, as countless and as soft as the hair on a human being's head. And from the seeds of all these plants, the Tree of All Seeds grew.

It was a magical tree! It rose from the middle of the ocean out of a single root. It had no branches and no hard and prickly bark, but was covered instead from top to toe with a sweet and juicy flesh. Right on top of the tree, the griffon bird made its nest. From time to time, the griffon bird would fly over the water, scattering seeds into it, which would then return to the earth through the rain.

Angra Mainyu, the Demon of the Lie, saw his evil acts being transformed miraculously into good. He was inflamed. Next to the Tree of All Seeds, a second tree had sprouted. This was the White Haoma Tree whose nectar was a powerful potion against old age, disease and death. He had been unable to destroy the first tree. Now he was determined to bring down the second.

Angra Mainyu created a poisonous lizard, which he placed at the root of the White Haoma Tree. 'This will eat into the roots and make it wither,' he thought spitefully, for he hated to see any living thing unless it was foul and fearsome. But in return, Ahura Mazda created ten great fish that surrounded the roots of the tree. Their heads faced the lizard, and their jaws snapped each time it came closer. They circled endlessly around the roots and kept the lizard away.

As if in celebration, a great mountain appeared between the two trees. It was a mountain with nine million nine hundred and ninety-nine thousand caves. From its nine million nine hundred and ninety-nine thousand caves streams of water poured out to revive the dying lands. The caves protected the water from Angra Mainyu's reach. He fumed and fretted but that didn't help. He had been beaten, and he knew it.

Smarting from his defeat, he decided to attack the Sole-Created Ox, the very first animal that Ahura Mazda had made. It was grazing peacefully by the river in the heart of the earth's seven lands, when Angra Mainyu descended on it in the form of a tiny fly. Disease, pain and hunger seized the poor creature like a curse, and its body fell lifeless to the ground. Its soul fled into the sky, weeping and lamenting. However, the body that fell to the ground became purified by the moonlight. From that purified seed a male and female animal arose. Two hundred and eighty-two species followed—pairs of every kind of four-footed animal, fleet-winged bird and silver-finned fish. Fifty-five kinds of grain and twelve kinds of healing plants sprang out. Peas grew where its horns had once been, and out of its heart grew thyme.

Now all this time, the first man created by Ahura Mazda had been living peacefully with the Sole-Created Ox. Formed out of the sweat of a prayer, Gayomart took the form of a fifteen-year-old boy, and opened his eyes to thank the Lord of Light for having created him. But when he opened his eyes, he felt as if they were still closed. In front of him, instead of the brilliant light he had felt in his mind, there was a night as dark as death. The planets were battling with the stars, the earth was covered with poison.

Angra Mainyu realized that Gayomart had awoken. He took the form of the Demon of Death and attacked him. But though Gayomart suffered terribly, he did not die till he was thirty years old, for that was what Ahura Mazda had planned for him. When he died, his body was purified by the sun and out of it arose eight kinds of precious metals—gold and silver, iron and brass, tin and lead, mercury and adamant.

Angra Mainyu saw Gayomart die and was happy. He thought he had destroyed man.

He was wrong. The gold from Gayomart's body remained buried in the earth, perfectly preserved in all its lustrous beauty by the Angel of Perfect Meditation. At the end of forty years a tender plant grew out of it. The plant had a single stem and fifteen leaves. But it was no ordinary plant. It was the first human couple in the form of a plant; the first man and the first woman with their arms entwined, so alike that it was hard to tell one from the other. Ahura Mazda breathed on them so they were filled with the soul that is the breath of life and He named them Mashya and Mashyoi.

'You are the first of mankind,' Ahura Mazda said. 'All future races depend on you, so live in perfect devotion. Do not worship demons. Do all your duties well, think good thoughts, speak good words and do good deeds.'

Mashya and Mashyoi looked at their Creator and were filled with joy. Then they looked at each other. The love they saw in Ahura Mazda's eyes was reflected in their own. Their first thought was to love and care for each other. Their first deed was to bathe in the pure clean waters of the earth. Their first words were that Ahura Mazda, Lord of Wisdom and Truth, Love and Light had created everything they saw. The water and the earth, the plants and the animals, the planets and the stars, the moon and the sun. He was the source of all good things, like love and happiness and well-being.

Angra Mainyu was filled with hatred when he saw that he had failed to eliminate man from the face of the earth.

'Go at once!' he ordered the demon Antagonism. 'Go to those feeble creatures and tell them the truth. It was not Ahura Mazda but I, Angra Mainyu, who created them and everything they see and adore so much!'

The demon appeared before Mashya and Mashyoi, who were only just beginning to breathe the sweet air and feel the soft breeze on their cheeks. Everything was so perfect and so real!

'It is all a lie!' the demon shouted, breaking their dreamy mood.

'What is?' they answered, feeling confused by the sight of this awful apparition, who looked like nothing they had seen so far.

'Everything you have been told,' the demon replied. 'Everything you believe is true is a lie!'

'How can that be?' they asked, timidly.

'Because Ahura Mazda doesn't want you to know who the real creator is!' the demon said, viciously.

Mashya and Mashyoi looked at each other. They were unnerved. Their faith, so strong just minutes ago, was already wavering.

'Who is the real Creator then?' they asked, dreading what his answer might be.

'Angra Mainyu!' the demon declared. 'Say it, or you shall die. Angra Mainyu is the creator of this wonderful world!'

Mashya and Mashyoi couldn't think straight. They were afraid both of the demon and the thought of their own deaths. They repeated, 'Angra Mainyu is the creator of this wonderful world.'

Hooting with joy, the demon returned to his master. Master and demon rejoiced.

But Mashya and Mashyoi were stricken. Ahura Mazda came flooding back into their presence and they knew that they had uttered their first lie and were to be punished. For thirty days they walked without eating a mouthful of food. Their garments were made of rough leaves and they walked barefoot. After thirty long days, they wandered, half-delirious, into a wilderness and found a white-haired goat. Mad with hunger, they rushed towards it, and drank its milk greedily. The milk was heavenly.

They walked on. After thirty more days they stumbled upon a sheep, which they slaughtered. The Angels took pity on them and taught them how to make fire out of the wood of the thorny plum tree. They built a fire and kindled it with date palm leaves, dry grass and fragrant myrtle and then they roasted the meat. In thanksgiving, they tossed a share of the meat into the fire and said, 'this is the Fire's share.' Then they tossed a share into the sky, saying, 'this is for the Angels.' A vulture appeared and carried away the piece they had tossed into the sky. They ate their first cooked meal, and they fashioned clothes out of the sheepskin that remained. They dug the earth with their bare hands till they found iron. They took the iron and they beat it with stones to give it a sharp edge. With this sharp iron blade they cut down a tree and made logs out of it. With the logs they built their first house and inside, they found shelter from the blistering sun. This was now their home, and they were glad.

But Angra Mainyu would not leave them in peace. He sent Demons of Hatred to make them quarrel. He sent Demons of Deceit who fooled them into making sacrifices to Angra Mainyu. But Ahura Mazda had not forsaken them for a minute. His hand was over them and soon a son and a daughter were born to Mashya and Mashyoi, followed by seven sets of beautiful twins, a brother and a sister to every pair. Ahura Mazda filled them with such tenderness and love that they forgot Angra Mainyu. They lived happily with their children, and taught them to follow Ahura Mazda, the Lord of Light, for all time to come.

But
one angel
did
not.

llah had just finished making the world. He looked at His handiwork and was pleased. The earth stretched out before Him, big and wide and beautiful. Out of that vast expanse of flatness, mountains arose. Some were steep and forbidding, their peaks glistening with ice. Some were gentle and inviting, their slopes covered with waving green grass. Sparkling down from the rocky peaks, streams of water ran into the fields. Rivers looped lazily through the plains. The air was filled with the sound of splashing and gurgling, rippling and bubbling. The earth was rich with growing things. Pairs of every kind of fruit hung juicily from the trees. There were big plump figs, bursting with sweetness. There were gleaming round pomegranates, their seeds red as rubies. There were luscious dates and succulent grapes. Vines curled, palms swayed, wheat rustled. Patches of differently coloured soil lay glittering crisply in the sunshine, a gay quilt of rich red, golden yellow, loamy black, silver white and burnt brown. Plants sprang up in every patch, watered by the rivers He had made. Depending on the soil they grew on, the plants were bitter or sweet, pungent or mild, thorny or velvety, delicate or tough. And just as the waters followed the slope of the land, night followed day. Like a cover over the day, Allah created the night, so that the world He had made could sleep under the soothing blanket of darkness.

Allah's angels couldn't stop praising what their Master had created.

17

'Never have we seen anything so wonderful!' they exclaimed. 'It is perfect! It is perfectly divine!'

But Allah knew there was one last detail that was yet to be completed. Only then would His creation be truly perfect. From among all His exulting angels, He called four to His side—Gabriel, Michael, Israfil, and Israil. Their wings shimmered. Their movements were graceful and majestic. Proud to be chosen by Allah, and ready for any task He might have for them, they waited for their orders. Allah, who alone knew what He was going to create next, commanded them to get Him handfuls of dust from the four corners of the earth. With a bow of their heads and a swish of their enormous wings, Gabriel, Michael, Israfil and Israil were gone. Hardly a few seconds had passed, when they were back. They offered the dust to Allah and with it He shaped a body. Arms, legs, shoulders, belly, everything was so finely shaped that even the angels were amazed. Now only the head and the heart remained, which Allah shaped out of sacred earth from Mecca and Medina.

The body of Adam was ready.

Like a potter makes a vessel, Allah had made Adam, the first man. He took the body, which He had still not breathed life into, and placed it tenderly outside the gates of Paradise.

The angels who passed by every day stopped to admire this new creation. 'What is it?' they asked Allah.

'Man,' Allah replied.

'What will be special about him?' the angels asked.

'He will be wiser than all of you.'

Hearing this, the angels looked at the silent form of Adam, and marvelled even more, that such a wingless and frail creature should mean so much to Allah and be set above them, and they praised Him to the seventh heaven.

But one angel did not.

His name was Iblis and he felt threatened by Adam. He looked long and hard at Adam's face, at his perfectly shaped body, at his noble expression, and he felt envy gnawing in his heart like a worm.

'What's wrong with the lot of you?' he jeered. 'Are you not angels, creatures of light? What makes you fawn over this hollow lump of earth, that can neither breathe, nor fly nor live forever? No, I do not find anything remarkable in this creature, and you who do are merely pretending!'

The angels paid him no attention. Iblis was always discontented. If he wasn't complaining about the span of his wings being smaller than Gabriel's, he was complaining about the weather. It was hard to please Iblis and nobody even tried. The creation of Adam had merely given him a new reason to sulk.

What they didn't realize was that Iblis's resentment went far deeper than that.

Meanwhile, Allah was ready to animate the body of Adam with a soul. He had already created the soul long ago, in preparation for this very day. A thousand years ago, out of the sea of glory that began and ended in Him, He had fashioned a living breathing beautiful soul. It was time for that soul to occupy its new home.

But the soul, which had got used to living in absolute freedom, with all the world to move about in, hesitated. Live in the narrow body of the clay figure! Exchange the infinite skies for such a cramped dwelling! She shuddered and seeing this Allah commanded her to enter Adam's body at once. 'Your hesitation shall be punished,' He said to her. 'Because you did not agree gladly to fill the body of Adam, one day you will be separated from that same body against your will and that day you will feel true pain.' He breathed on her, and she rushed through Adam's nostrils into his head.

Adam opened his eyes and saw Allah's magnificent throne. The soul reached his ears, and he heard the angels singing Allah's praises. She reached his tongue and he burst into praise for his Creator. The soul rushed into every part of his body, filling him with the warmth and energy of life, and when she reached his feet, Adam arose and stood before his Lord.

Allah blessed him and summoned all the living creatures of the earth before Adam. The beasts came, the birds came and the fish came. Allah taught Adam the names of each of His creatures. He told him how they had been created and where and how they lived. He told him the purpose of each of the creatures and how life on earth would flourish only if they were allowed to live in harmony and abundance. Then last of all, Allah summoned the angels.

'This will be my vice-regent on earth,' Allah said.

'Why him,' the angels said. 'He is made of flesh, he is sure to shed blood and make mischief, while we will only praise and glorify your name.'

'But,' Allah said, 'he knows more than you do.'

Pointing at all the animals and birds and creatures of the water, He commanded His angels to name them. The angels were silent. They knew how glorious those creatures were, but they did not know their names. And then Allah called Adam and asked *him* to recite all their names.

'That is a whale,' Adam said. 'And that a minnow. That large beast is a lion and that tiny creature a hare. The white bird is a heron and the pink one a flamingo.' And so Adam went on, fluently naming each of Allah's myriad creatures, not just in one language but in seventy different tongues.

'Now do you see,' Allah said sternly. 'He is wiser than you.'

The angels murmured in assent. Then Allah commanded them to bow down before Adam, as he was the only being animated by Allah's holy spirit. Israfil was the first to obey. One by one, all the angels stepped forward and bowed to Adam.

But one angel did not.

Iblis, who had hated Adam from the moment he saw his earthen shape, was filled with anger and disdain.

'I, an angel, bow down to a mere man!' he thought to himself. 'Never!'

And so he stood apart, determined to scorn Adam, whom Allah seemed to love so much. When Allah asked him why he would not do as the other angels did, Iblis replied with an angry toss of his proud head, 'I am made of fire! I will never worship one that is made of common dust!'

Seeing how haughty Iblis looked and hearing his rude and arrogant words, Allah expelled him from Paradise. The gates of heaven were to be closed to him forever. Iblis left, cursing.

Filled with wonder at the special way he was being treated, Adam thanked Allah and after eating a bunch of grapes brought to him by Gabriel, he sank into a deep and peaceful sleep. As he slept, Allah took a rib from Adam and formed a woman out of it, whom He named Eve. She looked exactly like Adam, except that her features were softer and more delicate than his, her hair was silkier and fell around her face in seven hundred long and shining braids, her voice was sweeter and her body finer.

While Allah was shaping Eve into the most beautiful creature on earth, Adam had a strange dream. He dreamt he saw a figure who looked exactly like him, but finer, lighter, sweeter and purer in every way. Who could this enchanting creature be? His longing to meet her was so strong that he woke up. And there in front of him was the creature he had dreamt of! Was he awake? Or still dreaming? In her eyes he saw the same wonder and love he felt in his own heart. Was she an angel? What was her name?

'Her name is Eve,' Gabriel said, reading Adam's thoughts. 'The Lord has made her to be your companion. Love her dearly and treat her at all times with kindness.'

Then Ridhwan, the guardian of Paradise, came up to them, leading Meimun, the winged horse, which he gave Adam, and a she-camel, which he gave Eve. With Gabriel showing them the way, they rode into Paradise. A tent made of green silk, supported by golden pillars awaited them. This was to be their home, and the whole garden was theirs to roam in. Delighted at how beautiful it was, Adam and Eve went for a walk, drinking in the miraculous sights and sounds of their new home.

Allah Himself came up to them and said, 'This garden will protect you from heat and cold, from hunger and thirst. Bathe in all the rivers, eat all the fruit, pluck all the flowers. Only one tree is forbidden. You may not pluck and eat the fruit of the Forbidden Tree. Do not break this one rule, and beware of the malice of Iblis. He hates you because he was expelled from Paradise on your account. He will do anything to make you suffer the same fate.'

Adam and Eve listened carefully, and for five hundred years they lived in utter contentment in Paradise, never once dreaming of breaking the rule that Allah had imposed. In fact, they were so happy, they had even forgotten about the Forbidden Tree. The angels observed their bliss and rejoiced.

But one angel did not.

Iblis had not had any peace since he had been expelled from Paradise. He haunted the gates, hoping to slip in unnoticed, but Ridhwan, the guardian of Paradise, never let his guard down for a moment. Torn by envy, maddened by impatience, he kept thinking of plans to destroy Adam and Eve, but was unable to carry a single one out.

One day, as he was hovering outside the gates, he saw the peacock coming out of the garden. Now the peacock was the most magnificent bird in Paradise, and he knew it. He prided himself on his rainbow-plumes, he flaunted the blue-green gold of his feathers, and he was completely conceited about his voice, which was so melodious that he had been chosen of all the birds to sing Allah's praises in heaven.

Iblis knew this very well, and a plan formed itself quickly in his cunning brain. When the peacock had strutted far enough away from the gate so as to be out of Ridhwan's hearing, Iblis appeared before the bird.

'Are you a heavenly creature?' he gushed. 'Never have I seen such a magnificent bird! Surely you must be from Paradise!'

The peacock puffed out his chest and fanned out his feathers with pride. 'I am. But who are *you* and where are you from?'

Iblis answered, in sugary tones, 'I am a cherub chosen to sing

Allah's praises without pausing. Only for a moment have I slipped away to get a glimpse of the Paradise He has created. Will you hide me under your wings and take me in?'

'Why should I do something that might upset Allah?' the peacock answered.

'In return I will tell you the magic charm that will protect you from illness, old age and death.'

The peacock, who had been too busy admiring himself all this while to really pay attention to Iblis, suddenly perked up. 'Death?' he said. 'In Paradise?'

'Yes, those who do not know the three magic words in my possession will die, even in Paradise.'

'Are you telling the truth?'

'Yes, I swear by Allah, the One and Only Creator!'

Hearing this, the peacock believed Iblis, for surely no one would swear falsely on Allah's name. He wanted to know the three magic words very much, but he was afraid of being caught.

'I cannot take you in myself,' he said to Iblis. 'But I will send you the serpent, who can move in and out far easier than me, who attracts so much attention!'

Now the serpent had been created a thousand years before Adam, and was destined to be Eve's friend and companion. She was a queen among beasts. Her green skin shone like emeralds and sapphires, her eyes held the fire of garnets, and her words were like music. The peacock assumed that she would be even keener than him to know the three magic words of immortality. He was right. When she heard that she might one day no longer exist, no longer glide jewel-eyed and imperious through the grass, she was filled with dismay.

'I will bring the cherub into the garden,' she thought. 'Let me go to him at once!'

She hurried outside and met Iblis. 'How shall I take you in?' she asked.

'I shall make myself small and hide myself in the hollow of your teeth,' Iblis answered.

The serpent agreed. She opened her mouth. Iblis flew in and settled on her tongue, poisoning it forever. She closed her mouth and glided past Ridhwan. Safely inside the garden, she opened her mouth, thinking that Iblis would emerge and take his own shape, but Iblis was too crafty for that. He stayed where he was, and urged the serpent to guide him to Eve's tent.

Reaching the silken tent, Iblis, hidden in the serpent's mouth, heaved a great big sigh. Eve, who was very fond of her sinuous playmate, looked up at once.

'What is wrong, my dear?' she asked.

'I am worried about you and your husband,' Iblis said, in a perfect imitation of the serpent's dulcet voice.

'But why?' Eve laughed. 'No one could be happier than we are! We have all that we desire!'

'What about the fruit on the Forbidden Tree?' Iblis said, slyly. 'You cannot have that, even if you desire it!'

'But we don't desire it! How can we, when we have so many other fruits to satisfy our hunger? What's one fruit compared to the riches of this garden?'

'That's just it,' said Iblis, heaving another enormous sigh. 'You have been granted all the fruits except the most important one!'

'And why is it so important?' Eve asked, still amused by the doleful words of her normally lively friend.

'Because, my dear, this fruit alone gives eternal life and vigour. The rest are only fleeting pleasures, this one is for all time!'

'And how do you suddenly know all this?' Eve asked.

'I met an angel under the Forbidden Tree,' Iblis answered, 'and he told me everything!'

'Take me there,' said Eve, 'so I can see if you are lying or speaking the truth!'

Iblis, knowing that his mysterious words would arouse Eve's curiosity, sprung out of the serpent's mouth, too tiny to be noticed by Eve, and before she arrived at the tree, he was waiting for her in the form of an angel with a human face.

'Who are you?' Eve asked, for she had never seen anyone like this before.

'I used to be a man, but now I am an angel,' Iblis answered smoothly.

'How did this marvellous thing happen?' Eve asked, her heart now racing with excitement.

'I was forbidden to eat this fruit by a jealous god, and so I withered away. I became so weak and disfigured, so bent and crippled that everyone would flee when they saw me. It was so bad that I began to long for death. Thinking that the fruit of the Forbidden Tree would bring me death, I reached out and ate it. At once, I became transformed into the being you see now. My limbs became strong and supple, my mind young and alert, and though a thousand years have passed since then, I have not changed, even a bit!'

'Are you telling the truth?' Eve asked.

'Yes, I swear by Allah, the One and Only Creator!' Iblis replied.

Eve's last doubts vanished, for surely no one would swear falsely in the name of Allah. She stretched out her hand, and plucked one ear off the wheat tree.

The Forbidden Tree in Paradise was a wheat tree. It was no ordinary tree. Its trunk was golden, its branches silver and its leaves were pure emerald. From every branch seven ears of wheat grew. Each ear contained five grains, each grain as white as newly-fallen snow, as sweet as honey and as large as an ostrich egg. Eve ate one of the grains. It was more delicious than anything she had ever tasted before. Filled with happiness, she took a second grain and offered it to Adam.

The minute he ate it, his rings fell off his fingers, his silken gown slipped off his shoulders and he stood naked before the Lord. The same thing happened to Eve, and they heard a terrible voice saying, 'Death and destruction is upon you! You are no longer fit for Paradise!'

Eve wept bitterly, as she realized she had been tricked. Adam's face grew pale. He tried to enter the tent to hide away from that terrible voice, but the tent closed before him and would not let him enter. He tried to climb on to Meimun, the winged horse, but Meimun reared up and would not let him sit. As they ran, hiding their faces, all the creatures of Paradise, who had loved them so much, shunned them.

Allah said, in His booming voice, 'Did I not forbid you to taste the fruit and did I not warn you about Iblis? Stand now and listen to your punishment!'

Adam was caught by the tangled roots of a tree, Eve by her own entangled hair. They stood and listened as Allah said, 'Everything you needed was yours for the asking. But now you will have to work for your food. This beautiful garden was your home for all time, but now the earth shall be your abode for a limited span only. Your hearts were filled with simple pleasures here. On earth you will be filled with pain and envy, illness and sorrow. The peacock will no longer sing in a melodious voice, but in such an awful screech that he would prefer to be silent. The serpent will be deprived of her feet and her charms, and will live in the lowly dust. As for Iblis, Iblis shall be cast into hell.'

No sooner had Allah uttered these words than they found themselves being hurled out of Paradise—Adam through the Gate of Repentance, Eve through the Gate of Mercy, the peacock and the serpent through the Gate of Wrath, and Iblis through the Gate of the Curse.

Adam and Eve found themselves on earth, and wept. The earth joined in their grief, and the creatures that had shunned them took pity and came back one by one. Feeling as if his heart would shatter into a million pieces, Adam cried out aloud, 'By listening to another I have sinned. You are our only God. Forgive us!'

Hearing these words of repentance, Allah shone His light upon them again. He sent His angel Gabriel as proof of His continuing love.

'Listen, O Adam and Eve,' Gabriel said. 'Live well, pray daily, do good to others, keep your heart free of sin, and at the appointed time, Allah will let you back into Paradise again.'

And so, Adam and Eve settled down to their life on earth. They lived as Allah had told them, looking forward to that wonderful day when the gates of Paradise would open and welcome them in again.

THE END OF
THE WORLD

The storm will be
beyond
imagination.

t was like any other day. Manu, the Sun's son, a great king, was making water-offerings to the gods. He bent down and scooped up a palmful of water, when a little voice broke into his prayerful thoughts.

'Please, great king, don't kill me!'

Now the last thing on the great king's mind was to kill anyone, especially someone he couldn't even see. He was so astonished he almost let the water slip back into the river, when he saw it.

A tiny fish wriggling on his palm. A fish with a voice as tiny as itself. 'Please, great king, have pity!'

A speaking fish, that too so small and helpless! Manu felt protective at once.

'Fear not, little fish,' he said. 'I'll put you into a little bowl, where you can swim about happily!'

And that is just what he did.

One day and one night passed. When Manu looked into the bowl again, he thought his eyes were playing tricks on him. Instead of the tiny fish he had rescued, a bigger, fatter fish looked up at him. What had been barely as long as his little finger was now at least a foot long! Its tail was sticking out of the side of the bowl, and its head twisting up towards him.

'Save me, great king! I cannot turn around in this bowl any more!'

'Yes, I can see you've outgrown the bowl!' Manu said, relieved that it was indeed the same fish. 'No reason to get worried, I'll just put you into a bigger one!'

The king ordered a large pitcher to be brought in at once. Carefully, with hands as gentle as only a kind king's hands can be, he transferred the now not-so-little fish into the pitcher. Bliss! The fish shook its tail gaily and did a fancy dive and a curly swirl. The king clapped. Great king and not-so-little fish were happy again.

But not for long. Early next morning, a piteous sound woke the king.

'Great king! Wake up! I cannot breathe in this pitcher! Help!'

'What? How?' Manu started up. He rushed to the pitcher and sure enough, not-so-little fish was now looking far-too-big. What had been one foot long was now ten feet long! The pitcher, which yesterday had been brimful of water, was now brimful of fish! One stuffed pitcher with one stuffy fish.

Manu put his men into action. They came, sleepy-eyed and rumple-haired, wondering at the king's new obsession. 'What's with the fish,' they grumbled to themselves. 'Why doesn't he just give it to us and we'll cook it. All this fuss and bother!'

But naturally, they didn't say a word. Obediently they carried the pitcher with the far-too-big fish to the nearest well, and *splosh*, emptied it into the deep dark water of the well.

'Thank you, great king!' Manu heard the fish's voice echoing out from the well. 'You are very kind!' And splish-splash, the fish was merry again.

Manu was beginning to see that this fish needed looking after. Who knows what would have happened if he hadn't visited the well the next day, just to say hello. The poor fish would probably have died for lack of water and the stone well would have broken with all its frantic tail-lashing and fin-thrashing. For that's what the fish was doing when Manu arrived. Lashing and thrashing about. 'Too small, again!' Manu thought, almost-admiringly. 'What a fish this is!' And without wasting even a minute, he had the fish transferred to a pond. For almost an hour it seemed as if the pond was the place to be, all round and roomy.

But no. Before the king's disbelieving eyes, the fish grew and grew and grew! He kept his men waiting, knowing he would need them any second now. The fish didn't even have to ask any more. Manu just saw, and acted.

The fish had grown three miles long. The pond was now no bigger than a fish-bowl. There were bigger ponds, yes, and lakes and bays and coves and lagoons. But Manu knew that the fish would outgrow them all. 'A river! A fast-flowing river,' he thought to himself, and had the fish put into the Ganges. No luck. The river shrank as the fish swelled. It was impossible to keep up. At last, not knowing where else to turn, Manu took the fish to the sea. The minute it slid in, waves whooshed, foam flooshed, and the air was filled with the spray and sting of water. When Manu could see again, he saw that the fish had filled the ocean!

He fell to his knees.

'I am a fool!' he said, passionately. 'A fool not to have known you at once! Forgive me, Kesava, for thinking you were but a fish!'

And in the impeccable way that kings have of knowing these things, Manu praised Vishnu by all his countless names, for Vishnu was who it was.

'What need for forgiveness, king?' Vishnu-in-the-form-of-the-Fish said. 'You have been wonderful and kind. No other king of your stature would have spared so much time and patience on a poor fish. Lord Brahma did well to grant you that boon.'

That boon! After all these years, that boon was to be fulfilled! Like water down a mountainside, the memory of it came rushing back to Manu. He had meditated once, for a whole million years. Brahma had been so pleased with him that he had granted him anything he wished for. And Manu had said, 'I want only one thing— when the end of the world comes, I want to be the protector of all its creatures.' And almost as if that was the most natural thing in the world, Lord Brahma, Grandfather of the World, had agreed.

But Vishnu-in-the-form-of-the-Fish was saying something. Manu came back to the present.

'The time is nearing,' Vishnu said. 'A great flood approaches. The earth and all its mountains, forests and plains will be drowned in a fantastic deluge. Nothing will be able to prevent the flood. But life itself will be prevented from vanishing. The gods have prepared a great boat, O Manu, to save all the living creatures on earth. And you are chosen to lead them all on board! You will be their captain, their saviour and protector. Everything that walks the earth, plumbs the deep and roams the sky will be under your care. The storm will be beyond imagination. But you will not drown. Just as you saved me when I came to you as a helpless fish, I will save you. And at the end of the age when everything else is destroyed, you will survive. You, the moon and the sun, the three godheads, the four directions, the holy books, the sciences, the river Narmada and the sage Markandeya will be the only survivors. The next creation will begin, and you will be its king. It will be called the Age of Manu, for you will be its master, worshipped even by the gods!'

It was a mighty big speech from someone Manu had first seen as a teeny little fish. So much had happened so quickly! Questions buzzed in his head. 'But when will this great deluge come? And how will I protect all the earth's creatures? And how will I know where to find you when I need you?'

It was a deluge of questions! But for Vishnu-in-the-form-of-the-Fish, nothing was too much.

'Listen,' he said. 'At first there will be a drought lasting a full hundred years, and then there will be famine. It will be a cruel time. Seven fierce rays of the sun will bring death upon the weak. The air will be filled with solar rays the colour of burning coals, multiplied seventy times by seven. Fire will erupt from the sea. Poison will flow from the nether worlds, and dissolve into flame as it flows. The third eye of Shiva will open and the three worlds will be burned to ashes. Space itself will be scorched by the terrifying heat and the entire world as we know it—with its men on earth, its gods in heaven, its creatures in the sea and its constellations in the sky—will be reduced to nothing.'

Manu, great king though he was, gulped.

'Into this great cauldron of smoking ash, seven rain clouds will bring rain,' Vishnu-in-the-form-of-the-Fish continued, blithely. 'Each cloud will have a name, wondrous names like Awful Roar, Thundercloud and Lightning Banner. As they let loose on the earth, the fire will be quenched, and great big clouds will form. A thick mist will rise. The rain will be so heavy, and fall so long, that the oceans will spill over to form one single gigantic sea. Such a huge sea will not be contained in one world. Under the never-ending flow of rain and sea, all three worlds will be merged into one single sheet of water.

'That is when you must gather the seeds of life from everywhere, and load them on to the boat, as carefully, as tenderly as you shifted me from one vessel to another. And then I shall come to your aid and you alone will not perish.'

And saying this, Vishnu-in-the-form-of-the-Fish vanished.

The only sound in Manu's ears was the whispering of the wind and the gentle murmur of the waves as they played at his feet. Who could imagine that these very waves would one day drown the world!

From that day on, Manu's life revolved around preparing himself for the flood. He did long hours of yoga, strengthening himself from within. Years went by. Finally, the day arrived.

Manu was ready. Using the power of his mind, he called all the living creatures to him, and loaded them on to the boat that had been built for that very purpose. And not a moment too soon. The rain clouds had burst, the winds were howling, and the waters were rising as fast as Vishnu-in-the-form-of-the-Fish had once grown before his eyes. All the creatures were safely on board. But on their own, they would never make it through the night, let alone through the ages before the next creation began. They desperately needed Vishnu's help. Where was the Lord, and when would He appear?

Before Manu had even completed this thought, Vishnu approached, a fish once again, but a horned fish. At his side was a serpent in the form of a rope. Manu fastened the boat to the Fish's horn using the serpent-rope, and bowing deeply to Vishnu-the-Horned-Fish, he stepped on to the boat at last.

Then followed an endless time. Or so it seemed to those on the boat. Waves as high as mountains swept over them, winds as violent as demons carried them far and wide. But all through, the rope that was the serpent held the boat fast to the horn of the Fish that was Vishnu, and Manu rode safely on the flood.

As they rode, Manu asked Vishnu-the-Horned-Fish all sorts of questions and he answered. Listening to stories—what better way to pass the time! And so Manu learnt how the world was made out of darkness, like that of a long and unbroken sleep. How Svayambhu-the-Self-Created appeared and scattered the darkness to the winds. He learnt how Narayana-the-Infinite-and-Eternal appeared and with him appeared a golden egg, shining like ten thousand suns. How Narayana entered the egg and became Brahma who made heaven and earth from the two halves of the egg. Then he made the sky, the eight points of the horizon, the mountains, the rivers, the clouds, the lightning, the Seven Seas and then finally emerged as the four-faced Brahma, Grandfather of the World, from whose thought the whole world and everything in it was born.

It was a journey to the end of time and also to its beginning.

They went a long, long way, northwards. Finally, Vishnu-the-Horned-Fish steered the boat to the top of the highest peak in the Himalayas and said, 'You will be safe here. Be sure to descend as the water subsides, and you will neither get washed away nor be left stranded on the mountain top. Goodbye.'

And with that he was gone.

The flood had swept away everything.

Manu was the last living man in the universe.

When the flood retreated, Manu climbed down from the mountain top. It was a dismal sight that met his eyes. Nothing remained. He and the creatures on the boat had survived, but the earth was dead. How would he, who had promised to protect the earth, bring it back to life? Knowing no other way, Manu threw himself into intense austerity. He fasted, he worshipped the gods, he performed penances, and finally one day, he made an offering of clarified butter, sour milk, curd and whey. Out of this rich and holy offering, a woman appeared before him.

'Who are you?' he asked her.

'I am your daughter,' she answered. 'I am your offering brought to life, the gods' blessings made real. Whatever you ask through me will be granted. Ask away.'

And so Manu invoked the gods through his daughter and was granted every wish. The earth was peopled with his children and the waters and skies were filled with living beings, just as it used to be. Manu ruled them all, and was called Prajapati, the master of all creatures on earth.

And he loved them all, but none so dearly as the fish!

It rained

without

stopping.

t was a time of great wickedness in the world. Men and women had everything they could ever want, and yet they wanted more. They lied and stole, hurt and killed, hated and destroyed one another. Seeing this, God's heart was filled with sorrow. His own creation, which He loved above everything else, made in His own godly image, was now turning monstrous and evil. What was beautiful was suddenly ugly, what was precious suddenly vile.

As He looked at them, grieving and regretting having made man at all, His sorrow turned into a terrible rage. 'I will destroy man,' He said. 'Man, and beasts, and all the creatures that crawl on the earth and all the fowls of the air.'

It was a terrible decision, but He knew there was no other way to make the earth pure again. But then as He watched and grieved and raged, He remembered Noah.

Noah was a man who had not turned evil.

In Noah, there still shone the goodness that God had put into man. He harmed no one, he told no untruths, he had no faults. It seemed that Noah was the last good man left on earth.

And so Noah was chosen to be saved.

God spoke to him and said, 'I am going to destroy the earth and all that lives on it. But because you, Noah, are blameless in a world marred by corruption, I will spare you and your family.

'Listen well. Build a great ark out of timber. It should be four hundred and fifty feet long, seventy-five feet broad and forty-five feet high. Put pitch on the inside and the outside. Make three decks inside and divide them into little rooms. Make sure you put a window in the ark and a door.

'Before I send the great flood, you, Noah, must enter the ark. Take with you your wife, your three sons Shem, Ham and Japeth, and your sons' wives.

'Also take with you into the ark two of every kind of animal on the earth, one male and one female, and two of every bird, one male and one female. Take food to last a long time, the kind of food that will sustain you and your family and the birds and beasts.

'After seven days, when the ark is full, I will open the floodgates of heaven, and it will rain for forty days and forty nights, until not a single living thing remains.'

Time passed. Noah built the ark just as God had instructed. Then one day, when Noah was six hundred years old, the rains came.

Noah was prepared. He led his family into the ark. Then two by two, he led the animals in. There were lions and lambs, leopards and fawns, elephants and iguanas. Predator and prey walked side by side, the big walked with the small. God had filled them with a mysterious sense of kinship that would allow them to live on the ark together. No animal was forgotten, from the shyest rabbit to the toughest rhinoceros. No bird was left behind. There were kingfishers and cuckoos, peacocks and parakeets, hummingbirds and hoopoes, black hawks and white doves. The ark was filled with twitterings and trumpetings, roars and rustlings, cawing and cooing.

Suddenly it all fell silent.

The door of the ark was closed.

And then the rain began.

It rained without stopping. The water rose and soon the ark was no longer resting on the earth but floating above it, a huge boat packed with life and dread and hope. The rain fell and the water rose. And with the rain and the water, rose and fell the ark. The timber made it buoyant, the pitch kept it watertight, but it was God's hand that kept it safe.

Outside, it was a cataclysm. Crops were flattened, trees were torn from their roots, villages were swept away and mountains were submerged. Animals ran amok, birds fell from the sky, men and women grabbed broken doors and fallen trees to try and stay afloat. But it was of no use. The rain still fell and the water still rose, and soon instead of air there was only water, so when the men and women and everything else that breathed drew great big gulps of air, all they swallowed was water, and so one by one they all drowned and died.

The only life that remained on earth was snug within the walls of Noah's ark. For forty long days and nights it seemed as if God had abandoned Noah. But on the forty-first, a great wind blew the rain clouds away, and the storm came to an end.

God had remembered the ark.

A terrible lull followed. Nothing moved, nothing stirred, the sun shone in impossibly empty blue skies and the earth emerged slowly from its watery grave. It took five months for the waters of the great flood to subside. On the seventeenth day of the seventh month, the ark found itself resting on the mountain of Ararat. Slowly, imperceptibly, the waters kept going down. Three more months passed. On the first day of the tenth month, the mountain tops could at last be seen.

Forty days later, Noah opened the window of the ark. A gentle breeze blew on his face and lifted his spirits. He picked up a raven from among the birds and let it fly out of the window. The raven, glad at last to have a chance to fly freely, went to and fro, looking down on the wet world, flying from one corner of the earth to another. When the raven didn't return, Noah released a dove. But the dove could find no perch to sit on and so she came back, and Noah took her in.

After a week had gone by, Noah sent the dove out again. That evening the dove returned, but this time she carried an olive leaf in her mouth. What a promising sign that was! The treetops were no longer under water!

But still Noah waited another seven days before sending the dove out again, and this time, when she failed to return, he knew that the waters had dried completely and that it would be safe for him to leave the ark.

And so, on the first day of the first month in Noah's six hundredth and first year, he removed the covering of the ark and rejoiced. The sun fell on his face with a warm and welcoming glow.

On the twenty-seventh day of the second month, God spoke to Noah, saying, 'Lead your family out from the ark. Then lead every other living creature out as well.'

Noah led his family out and then all the beasts and birds that had been saved. The skies were washed clean, the earth felt green and new, the whole world seemed as fresh and pure as it had been on the day of creation. Noah fell to his knees and gave thanks along with his family. He then built an altar to his Lord and offered burnt offerings at the altar, and God received them and was glad.

And God thought in His heart, 'Never again will I destroy the earth to save mankind. Never again will I put an end to all its living things. Instead, for all time to come, the earth shall be preserved, and day and night, summer and winter, planting and harvest-time will occur in never-ending cycles.'

And God blessed Noah and his sons Shem, Ham and Japeth, and told them to go and replenish the earth.

He said to them, 'From this time on, all beasts and birds, all creatures of the earth and the sea, will consider you their master. They shall be food for you, but only to fulfil your bodily hunger, not your hunger for sport. And if a man should take a man's life, men shall punish him. As a mark of this covenant that I make with you today, with you and with all future generations, I will send a rainbow each time I send a cloud. That rainbow will be a sign to you and a reminder to me never to send such a flood to the earth again. Now go forth and fill the earth with your kind.'

And so the animals spread to all corners of the earth, the giraffes and antelopes to the grasslands, the bears and snow leopards to the cold lands in the north, the lions and elephants to the warm jungles, and the dromedaries and kangaroos to the plains. Plants pushed through the green earth and birds hatched their young. The world was filled with life again.

And Noah? Noah planted a vineyard, and watched his sons' sons grow up and have children of their own. He lived for three hundred and fifty years after the flood, so that when he died, he was a Grand Old Man, nine hundred and fifty years old!

I see a
deadly
winter
in store.

n an ancient land, where the sun blazed golden and the rivers shone silver by the moon, there lived a man named Yima. In that age, time itself was measureless; it expanded and filled the heavens just as easily as it filled a single day on earth. When birds sang, human beings understood the words. When the wind blew, hearts beat faster. And when stories were told, they were never forgotten.

In such a time, and such a place, the Wise Lord, Ahura Mazda, spoke to Yima and said, 'Fair Yima, son of Vivanghat, you are a good man, as good and full of light as your father. I want you to spread my word among your people. Be my messenger and prophet.'

But Yima, who was as direct in his speech as he was truthful in his heart, said, 'I was not born, O Ahura Mazda, to be the teacher of your word. Command me instead to some other task.' He spoke fearlessly, as he knew that the Wise Lord would not be angry or offended by his refusal. He was right.

Ahura Mazda continued in the same kindly voice, 'Well then, be the guardian of my world instead. Nourish it, rule it, let it be filled with good things and good people. Let the earth flourish under your care.'

Hearing this, Yima replied eagerly, 'I will watch over your world well! I will make sure that while I am king, neither icy winds nor burning breezes shall plague the earth, and neither disease nor death shall harm its people.'

Ahura Mazda was delighted by Yima's heartfelt words. The passion He saw in Yima's eyes convinced Him that this was the role Yima was best suited to play. And so, to make the agreement formal, and to install Yima on the throne, Ahura Mazda gave him a golden seal and a magnificent dagger inlaid with gold that flashed every time he raised it.

For three hundred years, the earth prospered under Yima's rule. Flocks of geese and herds of cattle multiplied. Countless birds nested and hatched their young. Dogs gambolled and played at the feet of men, and contented families gathered around crackling fires each night. It was a happy time. As Yima had promised, there was no disease, and no death. Men, women, birds, dogs, flocks and herds grew so fast and lived so long that finally, one day, there was no room left anywhere on the earth.

What was to be done? Yima had a promise to keep and a world to look after. One morning, cloaked in light, he stepped out of his house and headed southwards, following the path of the sun. Reaching a likely-looking spot, he stopped and pressing the earth with his golden seal and marking it with his dagger, he said aloud, 'O Spirit of the Earth, do your creatures a kindness. Open at the point where my dagger rests and stretch yourself as far as you can to make room for your flocks and herds and men.'

Spenta Armaita, who was the immortal spirit of the earth, heard Yima's plea and made the ground open. The earth became one-third larger than it was. All the flocks and herds and men came pouring into the new lands and filled the earth which had grown larger for their sake, and so six hundred years passed under Yima in peace and prosperity.

But even six hundred years is not as long as it seems. Once again the earth grew too small, for the number of people and animals and birds had increased many times over. The earth had become so crowded that it was groaning under the weight of all its creatures. Once again, Yima marched southwards, following the path of the sun. Once again, he marked the earth with his dagger and said, 'O Spirit of the Earth, do your creatures a kindness. Open at the point where my dagger rests and stretch yourself as far as you can to make room for your flocks and herds and men.' And once again, Spenta Armaita listened and the earth grew two-thirds larger than it was. And so nine hundred years passed, joyously and abundantly, under the rule of Yima.

Ahura Mazda, who had been watching all this, and who had warned Yima each time the earth came close to bursting, called a meeting of the Celestials. He was worried, because floods and other disasters had accompanied each of the 'stretchings' of the earth. He called Yima, the good shepherd, as he was now known, to the meeting and he said, 'Listen well, O Yima, son of Vivanghat. I see a deadly winter in store, more numbing and more evil than anything before or since. The world will lie motionless under an unbroken frost. Snowflakes will fall thick and fast, till the world itself becomes an icy tomb and the highest mountains are lost under snowdrifts that are more than five feet deep. The wild beasts that live in untamed jungles, on unclimbed mountains and in undiscovered valleys will all seek shelter under the ground. The grass, so long and green and lush before the long winter, will die when the snow melts and the world exchanges its blanket of ice for a mantle of rushing water. At such a time, when all else is lost, imagine how wondrous it will be to see the footprint of a sheep on the ground!'

Yima was listening with amazement. He felt fear, but he also felt curiosity and anticipation. He knew the Wise Lord would never tell him of doom and disaster merely to frighten him. Ahura Mazda had a plan and Yima trembled to think that he would be the one to carry it out.

'And so, here is what you must do,' Ahura Mazda continued, as if reading Yima's mind. 'Build a *vara* underground, a strong square enclosure two miles long on each side, and into the *vara* bring the seeds of animals and birds and men and bring the red fire and make a haven against the storm.

'Inside the *vara*, dig trenches that are one mile long, and fill them with water so that they flow like rivers. On the riverbanks, let loose the birds, who will thrive in a land where the green never fades and the food never runs out, for that is how the *vara* will be. Build houses, each with a balcony, a gallery and a courtyard, and there bring the finest and fairest men and women, and the finest of all species of cattle.

'Then, O Yima, plant gardens, with the seeds of every kind of tree. Choose the very tallest like the cypress and the plane tree, and the most fragrant like the rose and the jasmine. Plant fruit trees—the most delicious like the date, and the sweetest-smelling like the orange. The very best of all these seeds you must bring into the *vara*, two of every kind, and they will bear fruit for as long as you are there.

'No one will be jealous, or spiteful in the *vara*, there will be no liars, no lunatics, no lepers, no one will be wicked or wayward.

'It will have nine streets, all beautifully laid out, and once you have brought in all I have told you, you must seal the *vara* with your golden seal, and make a door and a window that will be filled with inner light.'

Yima, who had been listening all his time without saying a word, now asked, 'But how, O Ahura Mazda, am I to make this *vara*?'

Ahura Mazda answered, 'With your hands, as a potter does. Break the earth and crush it with your heel, and then knead it as you would the potter's clay.'

And Ahura Mazda went away, leaving Yima to begin the formidable task of saving the best and finest of the world.

Yima, who was as bold as he was good, was not daunted by the magnitude of his task. He carried it out, just as he had been instructed, one step at a time. He broke the earth, kneaded it, built the *vara*, dug the trenches, made the houses, planted the trees, let loose the birds, herded in the flocks, laid out the streets and brought in the seeds of nineteen hundred men and women. Then, he sealed the *vara* with his golden seal, and made a door and a window that was lit up from within. It was a light quite unlike the one that lit the skies. It was not the light of the stars, the sun or the moon, and in the glow of that man-made light, a year seemed only as long as a day.

Yima lived in the *vara* with his people and his flocks and his herds. Every forty years, each couple gave birth to a healthy son and a lovely daughter and they all lived the happiest of lives, each growing a hundred and fifty years old. And while they were there, the heavenly bird Karshipta brought the faith of Ahura into the *vara* and taught the people to recite the holy verses in the language of the birds.

And so it was that when the great ice storm came, the best of the earth was preserved. Under Yima, the good shepherd, a hundred years passed in perfect bliss, until the time came when the snows melted, and the floods dried, and Yima and his people filled the cheerless earth again with their love, their life and their laughter.

THE DIVINE
CHILD & THE
EVIL KING

Then the
bad things
started happening.

had the misfortune of being Kansa's cousin. My father Devaka was his uncle, Kansa's dead father's brother. That made us first cousins, that close. But Kansa's father did not die a natural death, the poor man. His own son killed him, too impatient to wait for the throne that would anyway have been his. Mathura, happy glorious Mathura, became a city of fear after Kansa came to the throne so deceitfully. No one knew what he would do next, and everyone wished, in secret, that his reign would be short.

My poor father! He knew the only way to save his own family was to become the new king's ally. And so he asked Kansa to bless the marriage of his only daughter to Vasudeva, a noble member of our Yadava clan. That daughter was me, Devaki. Kansa saw nothing in this alliance that threatened him (being a man whose entire universe revolved around himself) and approved the match. The marriage took place with much pomp and glory. My cousin was in an unusually good mood at the wedding. Once it was over, he offered to drive us to my new home in his own chariot. I should have known nothing good would come of it. But my father had no objection, and so my husband (how strange that new word sounded to my ears!) and I got in, feeling slightly shy and unsure. We raced along. I was almost beginning to relax and enjoy the ride, when something unexpected happened. A booming voice burst out of nowhere, so loud and startling that we ground to an abrupt halt.

'You fool!' the voice bellowed. 'The woman you are escorting so happily to her husband's home is not as harmless as she appears. In fact, she is the precursor of your doom. Let her live and you, Kansa, will die! For it is her eighth son who is destined to put an end to you. Put an end to her at once, if you value your life, your kingdom and your throne.'

What? What was this outrageous voice saying? I looked shakily at my husband. Even Kansa was finding it hard to believe. This helpless woman his enemy? Her unborn son, his assassin? And then I saw his expression change from disbelief to a murderous certainty. Paralysed, I watched him lift his heavy sword out of his sheath. Paralysed, I watched him raise it. I would have died right then if my husband had not thrown himself at Kansa's feet.

'Please I beg you!' I heard him say, through the panic-haze that muffled all sound. 'Spare her! In return, I promise to hand every newborn child of ours to you. I swear it! Only let her live! With our children under your watchful eye, O King, surely no harm can come to your royal person!'

His words did it. I saw the heavy sword stop in mid-swing. I saw him lower it. My husband's words had pierced Kansa's hard resolve, seconds before the sword pierced my skin. I clutched the edge of the chariot. My mouth was dry.

'All right!' he growled. 'Your wife's life is spared. Such is the large-heartedness of Kansa that he keeps his would-be murderer's mother alive! Remember this, and remember you are forever in my debt. Driver, ride on!'

My husband thanked him, again and again. Secretly he held my cold and quivering hand. 'We are safe,' we thought. We shook with relief now more than with fright. Maybe Kansa was not as bad as everyone believed. Maybe . . .

Our thoughts were rudely interrupted. We had reached Mathura, but what was this? Instead of being dropped at the door of our own home, we found ourselves being thrown into prison. My cousin had spared us, yes, but he had no intention of letting us go scot-free, hatching all sorts of unsavoury plots behind his back. He intended to keep us confined, trapped, prisoners in a place where he could keep an eye on us, and make sure not one newborn child escaped. We clung to each other and cried. What a terrible homecoming for a bride!

Our first child was born. Instead of joy, all we felt was a deadening grief. Our precious firstborn to be handed over to that monster! But my husband had given his word. He gave the child to the guards, begging them to tell Kansa to be gentle with it. The guards laughed harshly and said, 'Gentle! We have been given orders to kill it, at once!' I fainted.

When I recovered, I saw my husband, sitting with his face in his hands, unable to speak. When he had offered to give our children to Kansa in return for my life, he had not dreamed that the king intended to destroy them. Fate was being cruel and there was nothing we could do.

Six children were born and six died. When the seventh child was in my womb, a miracle occurred. My child got transferred to the womb of Rohini, Vasudeva's other wife, who lived on the opposite bank of the Yamuna, in Gokuldham. Rohini gave birth to a baby boy and she called him Balarama. Our seventh child had escaped. But what would happen to the eighth?

Our eighth child was born at the stroke of midnight. The guards, normally so alert, were mysteriously asleep. The baby boy was beautiful and my heart was leaden at the thought of parting with him. Just then a vivid light filled our gloomy prison cell and we knew that this was no ordinary child, but the Lord Himself in human form.

The Lord said to my husband, 'Go now, under cover of darkness, to Gokuldham. There, at this very minute Maya has taken the shape of a baby girl in the house of the cowherd Nanda and his wife Yashoda. Place your son at Yashoda's side and bring the baby girl and lay it at Devaki's side. That way your son will be saved, and Kansa will be nearer his end.'

The light vanished, and my husband, full of reverence, picked up the tiny bundle and stepped out of the prison, whose gates opened by divine intervention.

Noiselessly, he crept out into the night. It was a stormy night.

Clouds covered the moon and stars, so that not a chink of light shone through. In utter darkness my husband walked, as swiftly and surely as if there had been lights blazing along his path.

At last he reached the river. It was in turmoil. Swollen with the rains, it threatened to overflow the banks and carry my husband and his precious bundle away. But knowing that he was carrying the Lord in his arms, he gained courage and stepped forward. Miraculously, the river stopped seething and the waters parted to let him through.

On the other bank, at Gokuldham, everyone was asleep. He tiptoed into Yashoda's house, picked up her little newborn girl, and with a longing look of farewell, placed our son where the girl had been.

Back in the prison, he carefully placed the girl in my arms. The sleeping child woke up and finding herself in a strange place, started crying. The cries woke the guards up, who rushed to inform their king that the dreaded child was born. Kansa couldn't wait for them to bring it to him. So keen was he to obliterate the eighth child of the prophecy that he arrived in the prison cell himself, casting terrifying shadows on the walls.

My husband joined his hands in desperate pleading, 'Please, spare her. It is a female child. What harm can a female child do?'

But Kansa would have none of it. All these years he had dreamt of this moment. Now to let it slip would be an act of immense foolishness. He picked up the child, and before our horror-stricken eyes, he dashed the child to the ground. Even the guards gave a gasp of shock.

But the child, who was really Maya, flew into the air in the form of an eight-armed goddess, a weapon in every hand, and laughed at Kansa. 'You fool! Your killer is safe and out of your reach. Repent your unforgivable deeds and swear you will not kill innocent children any more!' Saying this, she vanished.

The prison cell was silent and empty. Not knowing whether to rejoice that my eighth child was safe or mourn that my others were all needlessly dead, I hardly noticed what Kansa was saying. It was my husband who told me later, when we found ourselves in the open air, that Kansa had asked us to forgive him and then set us free. What could have happened to him? I didn't believe such a wicked man could have such a change of heart overnight. The clear night air filled my lungs. I had left the prison, but I couldn't shake off the fear that shackled my heart.

. . .

'Yashoda maiyya, you are blessed! Do you know what your son did today?'

'No!' I laughed, looking up from my work. 'What now?'

'He was sleeping under the wheels of our cart, and we feared he would get hurt. But instead, he picked up the fully-loaded cart and overturned it as if he were overturning a plate of sweets! What is he, a miracle?'

'Ah that he is, but a bad and naughty boy too!' I said.

There was no boy like my Krishna in all of Gokuldham, and I didn't say that just because I was his mother! The things he did! One day, I found him sitting with his mouth closed, his chubby fist curled around a lump of earth.

'You silly boy!' I scolded. 'What made you eat earth? Am I not feeding you enough malai and butter to make you fatter than Lord Ganesh? Open your mouth—aah!'

He opened his mouth.

I reeled.

I didn't see a lump of earth in his mouth, I saw the entire universe. Every little detail, down to me bending and looking into his mouth.

He shut it, and I stayed speechless. My son was divine. I couldn't move. And then he laughed his merry childish laugh and everything was like it was before, and I was running, running after him to make him wash his dirty little hands.

Then the bad things started happening. A she-demon arrived in Gokuldham. She was big and terrifying and called Putana. She rushed into the houses blessed with newborns and killed them. From far I could hear the voices of my neighbours weeping and wailing. I tried to hide but it was no use. Putana snatched my Krishna away and began suckling him. On her breast she had smeared a deadly poison that would have killed a grown man. I tried to take him back. The demon threw me off. Then I saw that my little lord was laughing. Laughing toothlessly and sucking the very life out of her! She shrieked and wriggled but Krishna would not let go. She shrivelled back into her ugly demon form and died, and my boy held out his arms to me.

I was relieved, but not for long. Another demon arrived, this time in the shape of a whirlwind. It was such a strong whirlwind that people, houses and cattle were lifted up like straws and blown away. I held Krishna tightly but he pulled out of my grasp and went running out. The demon picked him up. But before he could toss him away, Krishna clung to his neck and started choking him. He choked him and choked him till he died and at once the wind died too. People praised and praised my little one, but I was too afraid to rejoice.

That was when my husband told me what Vasudeva had told him: 'Beware of Kansa. He is afraid of your child and wants to kill him. Keep him safely!'

I scolded my husband for hiding this from me all this time. 'It was only to save you worry,' he said, meekly.

Only to save me worry! Two demons and who knows what else! 'We must leave at once,' I told him.

'Where?' he asked.

'Anywhere safe, somewhere the wicked Kansa cannot reach us so easily, somewhere hidden,' I said.

So we decided to go to the forest of Vrindavan. It was a lush forest, thickly wooded. On one side was the Govardhan mountain, on the other the Yamuna river. Rock, water and tree would protect our precious son. But we hadn't realized that the people of Gokuldham would not let us go.

'We can't bear to live without Krishna,' they said. 'Don't take him away from us!'

But we were firm. In the end, they decided to come with us. It was so, so strange, and yet so wonderful! The entire village moved with us to Vrindavan, and there we began a truly happy life.

But Kansa had longer arms that we thought. One morning, Krishna and his brother and best friend Balarama ran to the river to drink and found two of their cowherd friends lying unconscious on the shore. Krishna must have realized what was behind it, because he jumped into the river at once. Balarama shouted out in fright, but Krishna had disappeared by then. Balarama was so scared, he came racing back to get me. I ran to the river, and the others all ran with me.

There was no sign of my boy. The two unconscious boys still lay limp on the shore. Fearing the worst, we stared and stared at the still water. Suddenly it boiled and bubbled and a giant hundred-hooded snake emerged. Kaliya! Its purple fangs dripped poison and its black eyes glittered nastily. We screamed. Wrapped tightly in its slimy coils was Krishna!

The sky darkened, lightning flashed, the world groaned, the women swooned. But I looked on, and as I looked, a strange thing happened. The more the serpent squeezed, the bigger Krishna grew! He grew bigger and bigger, till finally it was he who was squeezing the serpent! Releasing his grip at last, he started dancing on one of Kaliya's hoods. The serpent was powerless. Krishna danced and danced till the blood came, and Kaliya breathed his last. The two boys woke up and when they were told of Krishna's tussle with Kaliya, they sobbed bitterly at having slept through it all.

A few days later, a bull followed, then a wild horse, but thank the Lord, each time Kansa's efforts at killing my boy were defeated, and the demons in their animal forms were killed instead.

There was silence for a while after that. We breathed easy. Maybe Kansa had given up after all!

And then the invitation came.

'His Royal Highness, King Kansa, would like to invite Krishna and Balarama to a wrestling tournament!' the royal messenger read out importantly, from a massive scroll. 'His Royal Highness has heard of the two boys' prowess and he would like to see it with his own eyes, and reward them richly. What answer shall I give him?'

Before I could say no, Krishna spoke up, cheekily, 'Tell him we'll be there, won't we, Balarama?' And the two boys laughed merrily. Merrily, as if they were talking about wrestling those other fool cowherds! I would have slapped him if the messenger hadn't been there. It was now too late to refuse.

'Well then, His Royal Highness will expect you!' the messenger said pompously, and left.

When I scolded them for putting their lives in danger by accepting the invitation, they only laughed and told me not to worry.

How could I not? The news that was trickling in was not good, not good at all. Kansa planned to put Krishna and Balarama into the ring against Chanura and Mushtika. Those two were the best wrestlers in the kingdom! They were tough and experienced men. They would break the two lads like twigs! Everyone joined me in warning them not to go, but the headstrong boys wouldn't listen.

What else could we do but accompany them to Mathura? The whole city had turned out to receive them. They lined the roads cheering, but that couldn't drown the banging in my head and the pounding in my heart. I had never been so afraid. And when we reached the gates of the stadium, my worst fears came true.

A mighty elephant stood at the stadium gate. Kuvalayapida was its name and it was known to be as mad as it was massive. The guards, when they saw the two boys approach, loosened the restraining chains that held it back. The elephant charged. The crowd fell back, yelling. But Krishna calmly sidestepped it and caught it by its tail. Enraged, it swung around and tried to gore him with its tusks. But the tusks broke in Krishna's hands and the mighty elephant came down with a crash. A cry went up from the crowd, a cry of jubilation, not of fright.

But this was just the beginning. As the crowd took their places, I spotted Kansa sitting in his royal box in his glossy robes, eager to watch two young boys die. Chanura and Mushtika stepped into the ring. The crowd gasped with pity and with fear. The difference between the two sides was heart-rending. The boys were so, so frail, and the men so fierce. But like me, the crowd had not realized how skilled the boys were. Within minutes, the two men were breathing heavily and losing their footing, huffing and puffing like a pair of clumsy beginners. Then, so fast that we almost missed the moment, Krishna and Balarama gripped first Chanura, then Mushtika by their broad and bullish necks and threw them down!

Seeing his biggest elephant and his strongest wrestlers reduced to a heap, Kansa lost his temper. He jumped up from his seat and ordered his guards to throw the boys in chains. He was so busy brandishing his sword and shouting, that he didn't notice how close by Krishna was standing. Before the guards could take a step in Krishna's direction, Krishna seized Kansa by the hair, dragged him into the ring and killed him.

You could have heard a bangle break! No one dared believe what they had just seen. Then the first cheer rang out. Then another. Soon, the air was throbbing, throbbing with claps and cheers. The two boys were heroes! I ran into the ring and after hugging them tightly, I made them swear, swear they would never be so foolish again. And then Devaki came running out of the crowd, and we embraced like long-lost sisters, and again we embraced our boys. It was a day of celebration. The prophecy had finally come true. Devaki's eighth son, my little Krishna, had killed the cruel Kansa. Mathura was a happy, glorious city once again.

He **forgot**
he was only
human.

he horrors of King Herod! Nobody knows for certain how many people he killed. Some books say fourteen thousand, others sixty-four thousand. You can take it from me, the books haven't a clue. I'd say the real number was more like one hundred and forty-four thousand deaths, and that too within just two years of the infant Jesus' birth. I should know. I was one of the men he used to wreak that trail of destruction. I have nightmares thinking of all the blood on my hands. I know my repentance will be long and my punishment heavy. I am prepared.

But to return to Herod. You may well ask, if Herod was such a bad man, how did he get to be king? To answer that, I need to go back to where it all began.

Herod's father Antipater was very friendly with the right people. That meant the Romans, who were then the most powerful people in the world. Antipater helped the Roman conquerors and in return, they helped him. One such helpful act was to make his son Herod the Governor of Galilee at the tender age of twenty-five. This early taste of power, that too obtained so easily, went straight to Herod's head. He saw himself as someone destined to be great, a natural-born leader of men, why even more—a king! In any other person, these thoughts might have remained mere delusions of grandeur, the kind of empty dreams that any ambitious young man might have. But in Herod, they were prophetic.

Eight years after he became governor, his powerful Roman buddies

Antony and Octavian asked the Roman Senate to give Herod the crown of Judea. Herod was over the moon. He went at once to the temple of Jupiter and thanked the Roman gods. The fact that the throne just given to him was still occupied by a hale and hearty Antigonus did not bother anyone. Three years later, Antigonus was beheaded—who knows at whose command—and Herod had the pleasure of occupying in person the seat he had so far occupied only in name.

In those days, kings married to increase their influence. Herod was no different. He chose Mariamne, daughter of one of the Hasmonean kings, who were then extremely popular among the Jewish people. (Herod probably hoped that some of that popularity would rub off on him!) In a fit of generosity, he made his wife's younger brother Aristobulus his high priest, but when he realized that this seventeen-year-old boy was a bit *too* popular, he had him killed. Popularity got on Herod's nerves. So did his wife's grandfather Hyrcanus. Like Aristobulus, Hyrcanus' only fault was that he had a way with the people. And so he had to die. Jealous of the Hasmoneans, Herod wanted them all wiped out. He wanted to be compared to no one. This was the strong king's greatest weakness.

What Herod didn't understand was this—you can win a throne by force, but you can't win people's hearts. Wiping out competition to make himself look more splendid in isolation, he also wiped out his last chance of becoming a king who would be adored instead of feared. Mistrust infected him like an incurable disease. He became as edgy as an iron saw and as jumpy as a cat. He looked over his shoulder constantly and had a dozen tasters taste his food before he himself touched it. One day, for no reason, he decided his wife Mariamne, and her mother Alexandra were against him. Blinded by insecurity and arrogance, he had them both killed. No price was too high for Herod when it came to buying himself a sense of unquestioned supremacy.

Any other man would have been haunted by guilt. Not Herod. Only one thing could frighten him—the thought of losing his crown. A few years later, when Octavian defeated Antony, the King of Judea was, for the first time, petrified. He had always been closer to Antony than Octavian. With Antony out of the way, would Octavian now try to overthrow him?

Reduced to a bundle of nerves, Herod travelled to Rome to meet Caesar, prostrated himself before him and swore his undying loyalty. Luckily for him, Caesar had no plans of awarding Judea to anyone else. Herod was a competent king, his personal life was of no interest to the emperor, and neither was Antony's fall from grace. No, Caesar had other things to think about. And so, instead of snatching Herod's throne from him, Caesar confirmed his right to be king of Judea. He even granted him more land. Herod was not only king, he was king of a bigger kingdom!

It was about this time that a disturbing piece of news reached him. I was in court the day the reports came in. It seemed that three men, travellers by the look of their long dusty robes and sunburnt faces, had been asking in Jerusalem for the new king of the Jews. These men, it was reported, said they came all the way from the East after seeing a sign that told them the king of the Jews had been born, somewhere in Judea. It was to see and adore him that they had come such a long way, and were in such a great hurry.

The king of the Jews? By rights that meant him, Herod, King of Judea. But he hadn't been born yesterday, he was an old hand. Much as he hated to admit it, they didn't mean him. Genuinely alarmed, Herod called all his chief priests and his scribes for a meeting.

'Tell me,' he asked them. 'Is what I hear true? Has there been born a new king of the Jews?'

The high priests and scribes were clearly nervous about telling the truth. Offending Herod was a dangerous thing! But their learning and piety bound them to the truth.

'Yes, Your Majesty, it is true. It has long been foretold by the prophets—that the leader of the people of Israel shall be born in Judea, and we believe that it has happened at last.'

'But where in Judea has this taken place?' Herod asked, beginning to sound tense.

'In Bethlehem, Your Majesty,' the scribes and high priests answered. 'Just as it was written by the prophets.'

It was a frightening thought that a mere prophecy might topple him from the throne!

'The three travellers—'

'Wise Men, Your Majesty,' said the chief priest, eyes lowered so as not to appear impudent.

'Yes, yes, the three Wise Men, if you will—I wish to speak to them. Bring them to my chambers and I will counsel with them in private. Let this be done at once!'

The three Wise Men were summoned to speak to Herod. They were fine men, tall, with flowing beards and faces that spoke of wisdom and courage. They had been told that King Herod himself had news of the miraculous birth, and they were eager to listen, not suspecting any other motive but kindness.

'Where do you come from, O Wise Men?' Herod asked, warmly, for he could be warm when it suited him.

'The Far East,' they replied. 'Far have we travelled and long. Ever since we saw the star that told us the Lord has come, we have not taken our eyes from the sky. Hunger, thirst, weariness, nothing has been able to turn us from our path. It was a sign from the Creator Himself and we were blessed to have seen it.'

Herod, who didn't enjoy being reminded that there was a Creator far superior to him, bit back his annoyance.

'And how did you know you should come to Judea?' he asked.

'The star led us here,' they answered. 'In Jerusalem shall the king be born, we were told. But having come so far from home, and so close to our destination, we seem to be at a loss. The star stands still in the sky and our hearts grow impatient to see the king and adore him.'

If Herod had his own way, the only king worth adoring would have been him. But he had to be subtle and not give away the dark designs behind his seeming kindness to the strangers.

'Ever since I have heard the news, O Wise Men, I am no less impatient to adore the infant lord than you are,' he said. 'My priests tell me Bethlehem is where he is born, it is what the prophets have said, and surely prophets cannot be wrong! Go then to Bethlehem and when you have found him, come back to me with news, so that I too may go and adore him.'

The Wise Men bowed, and left the court. The star that had stood still all this time went ahead of them, an immense light that drew them on, on, till it finally stopped over a barn.

Now you may well ask how it was that the king of the Jews, saviour of his people, came to be born in a barn. Well, this is how it happened.

· · ·

We had been walking a long time. It was a strange city, and if my husband had not insisted we make the journey, I would never have come.

'Caesar has sent out a decree that we are to be taxed, each in the city of our birth,' my husband told me. 'You know I belong to the house of David. And the city of David is Bethlehem. Come, we must go to Bethlehem at once.' And so we went.

In my womb, the divine child seemed almost ready to be born.

'It is a vision I have seen,' my husband had told me. 'An angel appeared in my dream and said, the Son of God will be born to your wife Mary, and you shall name him Jesus.' I had felt a little scared ever since, and also a little proud.

But as we walked and walked, our work with the taxmen over, all I felt was tired. The whole country seemed to be in Bethlehem! Everywhere there were men with their families and children, roistering young lads with red-cheeked lasses, talk, bustle and gaiety. Not a single inn had room. No, sir, sorry, everything's taken. My husband pointed towards me, as if that would make the innkeepers change their minds, but it was no good. After a point they stopped talking, just slammed the doors in our faces. Once in a way, but a very long way, a kinder one would give us an address we might try. But still, no luck. I was near weeping with exhaustion and anxiety. I yearned to be back home, in my soft bed, my own mother next to me with her kind and loving face. The divine child coming and I still feeling like a child myself! And then suddenly, when I had given up all hope, a man took pity on us.

'If you do not mind sharing the barn with the cattle,' he said to my husband, 'you and your good woman can take shelter there. There is plenty of fresh hay, and a lamp to keep you warm.'

It was a humble barn, but to me it was the grandest palace in the world! Fresh straw was scattered on the floor, and there I lay, grateful for the rest at last. That night, the divine child was born. Cattle lowed gently all around us, and the lamp flickered cheerfully. Happy beyond words, I held my babe close. And that is how the Wise Men found us.

I wondered if I was dreaming. Bending their tall frames, they entered through the door, out of the black night. Their faces were grave and humble. To my surprise, they fell to their knees when they saw us. Their joy, like mine, was beyond words. After kneeling and worshipping the babe, they opened their travel-stained bags and brought out the most precious gifts. Gold, that seemed to glow brighter in the radiance from my sleeping child's face. Frankincense, that filled the hut with its sweet perfume; and myrrh, that was filled with the promise of things to come.

I fell into a deep, untroubled sleep. It wasn't morning yet when I found my husband shaking me awake. 'It is a vision I have seen,' he whispered. 'The angel came to me in my dream and said, "Fly, take Mary and the divine child and fly to Egypt. You are not safe here. King Herod is looking for you and when he finds you he will destroy the child. Hurry! Remain in disguise till I tell you it is safe to return."'

What ill news! I got up at once, and holding my child tightly to my breast, I followed my husband to Egypt. It was the dead of night, and the three Wise Men were nowhere to be seen.

The three Wise Men never returned. Story has it an angel told them to go back to their homeland by another path, under cover, unknown to King Herod and his spies. Herod, who had been waiting impatiently for news of the child, was incensed when he realized they were not coming back. He had been tricked. A baby was being worshipped instead of him! A puny weakling child was the challenger to his kingship! It was unthinkable and he would have none of it.

White-lipped with fury, red-eyed with revenge, King Herod summoned his cruellest, coldest men. Us.

'Go!' he ordered. 'Go to Bethlehem, and seize every boy-child that is two years old and younger and kill it. Show no mercy, heed no grieving mother's tears. Leave no house in and around Bethlehem un-searched. If even a single boy-child is left alive, I will cut off your heads!'

And so, obedient servants that we were, we went to do his bidding.

I will never forget that sound—the sound of weeping. For the next few months, Bethlehem was a city of wailing women. They tore their hair, beat their breasts, and fell at our feet. 'Spare the innocent babes,' they pleaded. 'Show mercy! God will bless you for your kindness!'

Their pleas fell on deaf ears. What concern was it of ours that Herod should want to kill innocent babes? He had killed his own children, had he not? Suspicious of a plot against him, he had raised not his fist, but his sword and slain his two young boys. A man who had no mercy for his own children, what mercy would he show to the children of others? We were not to be blamed. We were just doing our job. We had our own lives to save, our own families and children to think of. And so, trying to explain away our heinous crimes with such feeble excuses, we found and slaughtered all the two-year-old boys in Herod's kingdom.

Hell is too good for me. How many nights I have woken up screaming, just thinking of what I have done.

But this story is not about me. King Herod was so relieved that the 'pretender' to his throne had been exterminated, that he was lavish in his praise and generous with his gifts. He rewarded us royally, and freed from worry and fear, he went back to doing what he did best—terrorizing his people and glorifying himself.

So vain had he become that he forgot he was only human.

A dreadful disease struck King Herod and he retired to a town by the Red Sea to recover. Convinced that the illness was a conspiracy against him, he sent a letter to Rome asking permission to execute his favourite son, Antipater. It is said that when Caesar received the letter, he remarked, 'It is better to be Herod's swine than his son.' It is also said that during those last days, Herod's happiest hour was when the letter from Rome arrived, allowing him to kill Antipater. Five days after it was done, Herod himself was dead.

Now Herod, while still alive and ailing, had instructed us to have all the leading citizens gathered in a hippodrome in Jericho and killed the day he died. His reason for this peculiar instruction was as simple as it was twisted. He knew, in his heart of hearts, that no one would mourn his death. (Even Herod couldn't hide that fact from himself any more.) But if the kingdom's finest men were to die on the same day, then at least *their* families would shed tears, and the air would be filled with the kind of lamentation that should have been his due. But his hold over us was over. We ignored his order. Instead, we opened the state coffers and threw coins into the street. We danced with our women and kissed our children. I laughed and wept and prayed. I could repent and hope to be saved. I was free at last. The tyrant Herod had fallen at last.

I felt it in my bones. It was time to take Jesus home. And I was right. That night, the angel appeared in my husband's dream and said, 'Joseph, Herod is dead! Take Jesus and Mary and return to Israel!'

And that is just what we did. Hearing on the way that Herod's only remaining son, Archelaus reigned in his place, we decided to go to Galilee instead. There we settled in the city of Nazareth, and my son grew up as a Nazarene, free at last to follow what destiny had in store. My cup of joy was full.

THE PRINCE
WHO GAVE UP
THE EARTH

Softly,
silently,
the massive gates
began to
open.

This is the story of a prince who could have been king. Instead—well, this is the story of what he became instead.

His father, my king, was Suddhodhana, lord of the Sakhya clan. The Sakhya kingdom lay at the southern foothills of the Himalayas, along the gentle river Rohini. Its capital was Kapilavastu and there was never a more beautiful city. King Suddhodhana was a good king, his subjects loved him, his clan respected him, and the neighbouring kings treasured his friendship. Everything would have been perfect but for one small fact.

King Suddhodhana and his wife Queen Maya had no children. No laughing voices filled the royal gardens, no little feet pattered behind the queen and her maids, no heir filled the king's heart with pride. It was the cause of great sorrow among the people, though they never expressed it, and even more so to the royal couple. I was then a small boy, a groom at the king's stables, but even I could tell that the king and queen were unhappy.

Twenty years went by. I was now the king's charioteer and I enjoyed his special favour.

It was the seventh day of the Midsummer Festival that Queen Maya had the dream that would change everything. For seven whole days the entire city of Kapilavastu had been celebrating. On the last day of ritual and revelry, Queen Maya distributed four hundred thousand pieces of gold to her people, and finally retired to her chamber to sleep.

As she lay on her couch, she dreamt that four resplendent beings who were too brilliant to even look at, lifted her up, couch and all. They carried her to the Crimson Plain in the Himalayas and put her down gently under the giant sal tree that was seven leagues high and one hundred and forty leagues wide. Their four queens took her by the hand, bathed her in a heavenly lake and dressed her in glimmering clothes. Garlanded with flowers, she was led to a silver hill, on which there stood a golden mansion. Inside was a glorious couch and there she lay down. It was so soft, she felt as if she were floating. She then saw an even more wondrous sight. A great white elephant, with great white ears and a silver-white trunk approached her. In his trunk he held a pure white lotus. He bowed down low before her and uttering a single unforgettable cry, he gently struck her on the side with his dazzling ivory tusks.

The next morning, when Queen Maya awoke, she remembered every detail of her dream. She told her husband, King Suddhodhana, and he marvelled, but was unable to say what it meant. So he called sixty-four learned Brahmins, served them delicacies out of gold and silver bowls, showered them with gifts, and asked them about the dream.

The Brahmins seemed to know at once. 'It is simple, Sire,' they told him. 'The queen is about to have a boy-child. No ordinary child either, but one who will become either a Great King or a Great Saviour.'

The moment these words were spoken, thirty-two good omens occurred. The blind began to see. The lame began to walk. The dumb spoke and the deaf could hear. Chains fell away from prisoners. The fires of hell went out. Men were kind to one another. Musical instruments played all by themselves. The clouds cleared. The salty seas turned sweet. Lotuses rained down from the sky and bloomed out of rocks. And unknown to her, four *devas* with swords in their hands stood guard over Queen Maya, to protect her from all harm.

The king was beside himself with joy. 'Channa, this is a day I will never forget!' he told me as we went on our evening ride. 'Here, take this gold and buy your wife a wonderful gift!' The entire city rejoiced, and for weeks no one talked of anything but Queen Maya's dream and what it meant.

The queen decided to have her baby in Devadaha, where her family lived. As she travelled there in a golden palanquin, accompanied by her retinue, she passed Lumbini where the most beautiful sal grove stood. The branches were heavy with fruit, and flowers of every colour imaginable filled the grove with perfume. Birds warbled as she passed. Suddenly the queen was filled with the desire to sit for a while in the grove. Her attendants carried her in, and placed her under the stateliest tree of them all. The green canopy above her was spangled with light. She reached out to hold one of its beautiful branches, and just then her baby was born.

The very next day, an ascetic arrived at King Suddhodhana's court and said, 'Let me see your newborn son, O King.' The boy was brought before him. The ascetic took a good look at him and burst into tears. Everyone was alarmed. Did some dreadful misfortune await the king's heir?

'Oh no,' the ascetic said. 'I do not weep for the child, but for myself. My joy at seeing him is boundless. But my greatest sorrow is that I will not live to see this child save the world from ignorance and suffering.'

Now, the king, who was euphoric at his son's birth, could not help but get a little worried by all the prophecies that were being made. Surely his son would not renounce the world? Or would he? To put an end to all his doubts, he called one hundred and eight Brahmins and asked them to tell him once and for all what the child would grow up to be. Eight of the Brahmins were skilled at recognizing signs.

'If he remains a householder, he will become a Universal Monarch, O King,' they said. 'But if he forsakes the world, then he will become an Enlightened One, a Buddha.'

The king was deeply troubled. 'What will make him forsake the world?' he asked.

'The four omens,' they replied.

'Which four omens?' the king asked.

'An old man, a sick man, a dead man and a monk.'

'Then I will never let him see any of those things!' the king declared.

It was only natural. 'After all these years, a son is born to me, Channa!' he said to me as we drove to his pleasure gardens that evening. 'What a waste if he gives up everything and becomes a holy man! No, I want to see him ruling the four seas, the four continents and all the islands in between. I want to see him commanding millions, walking on earth as if in heaven, surrounded by countless courtiers and wise men!'

I nodded in agreement, for which king would not want his son to outdo him in his glory!

And so King Suddhodhana had high walls built around the palace and placed guards two miles apart in all four directions to prevent his son from seeing any of the four signs that would tear him away from worldly ambition.

Our prince was named Siddhartha. It was a good name, it meant 'one whose goal is fulfilled'. Sometimes I wondered—whose goal would Siddhartha fulfil in the end—the one destined for him by the gods, or the one chosen by his father? No one could tell.

One day, when he was still a child, during the Ploughing Festival, his nurses were amazed to see the little boy sitting perfectly still under a jamun tree. He was holding his breath and meditating with his legs crossed under him. As long as he sat, the shadows of the other trees lengthened and shortened, but the shadow of his own tree never changed its shape. The nurses told the king, and the king was afraid.

Time flew. Our prince grew up to be a very handsome young man. He was taught the usual princely skills, but he was also pampered excessively. He never stepped anywhere without someone holding a white parasol over his head. Neither heat nor cold, dust nor dew, falling leaves nor gusty winds were allowed to ruffle his delicate frame. He wore only the finest garments of muslin spun in Kashi. Three lotus ponds were built specially for him, one with blue lotuses, one with red and the third with white. Three palaces were built for him, one nine storeys high, one seven storeys and one five. He spent the four months of summer in the first palace, the four rainy months in the second, and the four cold months of winter in the third. In each of them, the king surrounded him with beautiful dancing girls, who played music, sang songs and entertained the young prince. At the age of nineteen, like any father would, King Suddhodhana married him off to a lovely princess called Yashodhara.

But not everyone loved him unconditionally. His clansmen resented the fact that the young prince was only interested in having a good time, and complained to the king.

'Siddhartha seems to have devoted himself to a life of pleasure,' they said. 'What if war is declared? Will he be able to lead our soldiers against our enemies?'

'I told Siddhartha what they said,' the king said to me proudly, as we raced to the tournament hall. 'And he laughed gaily and said, "Father, let them all come, all the skilled men in our kingdom, and see if I can't silence my critics!" What a boy he has grown into, Channa, what a kingly boy!'

And I nodded, but I was afraid, in case our young prince had agreed to take on more than he could handle.

I feared in vain. At the tournament, Prince Siddhartha wrestled and shot and fenced like a hero! He was better than the best archer for he could split a hair in two with his arrow, and he was faster than those who could shoot as fast as lightning. In twelve military skills, he took on every single opponent and defeated him. The crowd cheered like crazy and his clansmen doubted him no longer.

One day, feeling restless and bored inside one of his palaces, Prince Siddhartha decided to go for a ride. After his grand success at the tournament, the king had gifted the prince his best chariot and with it, his favourite charioteer. I was now at the young prince's command. 'Make the chariot ready!' he called out. I did so at once, yoking the four majestic horses that were whiter than the whitest lotus. We rode out into the fresh evening air.

As we rode, the prince saw a strange sight. It was a man hobbling along with the help of a stick. His hair was white, his back was bent and his teeth had fallen out. Never before had our protected and pampered young prince seen anything so strange and awful.

'What kind of a man is that, Channa?' he asked me.

'An old man, my Prince,' I replied. How had an old man come so close to us? The king had forbidden it!

'Old?' the prince asked, for he had no idea what that meant.

'One who has lived for many years, my Prince,' I told him.

'Will I become an old man too one day?' the prince inquired.

'Yes, it is the fate of all men. All who are born must one day become old,' I said.

The prince thought about this and was shaken.

'What good is it then,' I heard him say to himself, 'to take so much pride in being young?'

We had hardly gone a bit further when he saw something else he had no name for. It was a pale man, very thin, whose wasted fingers shook uncontrollably as he tried to wrap his shawl around himself and whose breath came with a terrifying rattle.

'What is wrong with this man, Channa?' Siddhartha asked. There was panic in his voice.

'He is ill, my Prince,' I replied, quelling my apprehension.

'Ill? And what does that mean?' asked the prince who had never been sick in his life.

'It means when your body is no longer healthy, and is full of pain.'

'Pain!' the prince repeated. His voice was oddly heavy. 'Does pain happen to everyone?'

'Yes my Prince. It is only natural to fall ill and feel pain.'

'What good then, Channa?' he said despairingly, 'to be so proud of being healthy?'

There was more to come. A little while later, the prince saw a group of men carrying a man who lay stiff and cold on a stretcher.

'What has happened to him, Channa?' Siddhartha cried.

'He is dead, my Prince,' I answered softly. 'He has reached the end of his life. That is what lies in store for all of us.'

'Alas!' the prince sighed. 'And here I am so proud simply because I am alive!'

We drove on in silence. I could tell from the way the prince sighed and shifted uncomfortably in his seat that he couldn't stop thinking of all he had seen. Why had he not seen any of it before? I could tell he wanted to rush back to the palace and hide himself among his dancing girls and his princely pursuits. But something prevented him.

'Stop!' he suddenly cried. 'Stop! Who is that?'

I halted. The prince was pointing to a man who sat peacefully by the wayside. He wore a simple robe, his head was shaved, and in his hand was a plain wooden bowl. Eyes closed, the man sat, a look of pure contentment on his face.

'What has he got that makes him look so happy?' the prince asked me.

'Nothing, my Prince,' I answered. 'He has given up everything, his possessions, his family, his desires. He is a monk.'

The prince fell silent, as if all his doubts had been removed.

He did not know it, but the four omens sent by the *devas* had been seen. The wheel of fate had begun rolling, and no one could stop it now.

It was late by the time we returned to the palace. The air echoed with music and merry voices. Women sang and danced. 'A son has been born to Prince Siddhartha,' they sang. 'What a glorious day! Blessed is King Suddhodhana, doubly blessed in his son and grandson!' Golden lamps gleamed from every corner so the palace looked as if it was bejewelled with light. Incense filled the inner chambers. The stars themselves seemed to dance with joy.

The prince hardly noticed. He dismounted and went in without saying a word. My own heart was torn in two. One part of me grieved to know that the prince would leave the palace, and break his father's heart. Another part of me rejoiced, for I was witnessing something special. What a terrible burden for a twenty-nine-year-old to carry, I thought, as I watched him go. To leave not just his way of life, but also his dear wife Yashodhara and his newborn son Rahula.

That night, instead of retiring to my own quarters, I decided to sleep outside the prince's room. I had a feeling he would need me. In any case, I couldn't sleep. And from the sound of footsteps walking to and fro behind the closed door, it seemed the prince couldn't sleep either.

When the rest of the palace had quietened down at last and all the revellers had collapsed with exhaustion right where they were,

I heard his door open. Before I could get out of the way, he stumbled over my legs.

'Who is it?' he whispered, almost angrily.

'It is I, Channa, my Prince,' I said, getting up hurriedly.

'Good. Saddle my horse at once,' the prince said. 'But do it quietly. Tonight I am leaving.'

My heart leapt. The time for the great renunciation that the Brahmins had predicted had come.

I went to the stables and saw Kanthaka, the prince of horses, white as the snows, pawing the ground impatiently with his great hooves. 'You will carry my master tonight,' I whispered to him, and saddled him swiftly. Kanthaka neighed loudly with joy. I tried to hush him for I didn't know that no one would hear him, that they all slept soundly under a spell woven by the *devas*.

'Your horse is ready, my Prince,' I said, going back inside.

'Give me a moment,' he said, and tiptoed towards Yashodhara's chamber. 'I will take just one look at my son, one look before I leave.'

Softly, he opened her door. I looked away, trying to hide my tears. I could picture the scene as if I were saying goodbye to my own wife and child.

The room was lit with an oil lamp. The flame flickered and lit up Yashodhara's face as she lay sleeping on a bed strewn with jasmine flowers. She breathed softly and her hand lay gently on her son's head.

'If I pick him up to kiss him, she will wake and then I will not be able to do what I must,' he thought. And so, shutting the door as softly as he had opened it, he left the palace.

There were tears in his eyes but no one saw him shed them except me.

He leapt easily on to Kanthaka's back and, with me riding behind him, we arrived at the gates of the city.

Now King Suddhodhana was so afraid of losing his son to a hermit's life, that he had placed a thousand men to guard each city gate. Each gate was impassable, high and strong and spiked. A single man would never be able to swing it open. And even if he could, the noise alone would have woken the guards. If the guards awoke, the prince would be taken right back. I don't think the prince realized until this moment how difficult getting away really was.

'Listen!' he said to me in a low voice. 'I am going to jump over the wall. Kanthaka will be able to do it. You stay behind. Goodbye!'

He was just about to whisper an order into his faithful Kanthaka's ear, when softly, silently, the massive gates began to open. No one stood behind them. My jaw dropped. It must have been the *devas* at work, their strong invisible hands pulling open the gates so my prince could go where he must.

But one more obstacle remained. Mara, the tempter, appeared before us and said, 'Prince Siddhartha! Stop! Do not leave this way, like a thief in the night. It is not befitting of a king! In seven days, the treasure-wheel will appear and make you sovereign of the four continents and the two thousand islands in between. Stay! Stay and enjoy what is your due!'

Mara was very clever indeed, hoping to appeal to the young man's sense of pride and ambition! But my prince was not so easily swayed. He ignored Mara and continued riding.

This riled Mara no end. 'No one ignores Mara!' he snarled. 'I will not let go so easily. Wherever you go, I will follow like a shadow, and whenever an angry or an evil thought crosses your mind, I will show myself and tempt you!' Saying this, he darted behind us, a dark shape full of evil and hate.

It took me a while to shake off the unpleasant sensation that Mara had caused. Only then did I realize what a beautiful full-moon night it was. As my prince rode away from the city of his birth, his boyhood and his youth, he felt a strong urge to look back at it once more. But before he could rein Kanthaka to a halt, the earth's movement itself halted, so that the Buddha-to-be could gaze at the city that was no longer his. He gazed for what seemed an endless moment.

'Isn't it strange, Channa?' he said, when we were riding again. 'I thought I would be sad but I am not.'

In the space of that one night, we passed through three kingdoms. At last, after thirty leagues, we reached the banks of the river Anoma. The prince pressed Kanthaka gently with his heel, and the horse sprang across the wide river in one leap and landed softly on the opposite bank.

The sand was gleaming like silver. It stretched endlessly on either side of us as we stood. The prince got down and said, 'This is where we must part ways, Channa. Take my ornaments and Kanthaka, and go back to Kapilavastu.'

I am not ashamed to say it. I wept. I had come this far with my prince, I wanted to go even further. 'Let me renounce the world too, Master,' I said to him. 'Let me follow you everywhere, and be your servant.'

But he would not have it. One by one, he took off his princely ornaments and his fine-spun robes. Now only his long plaited hair remained, with the crown prince's diadem on his brow. 'These too must go!' he said and with his sword he cut off his locks. Head shaven, clad in a rough robe, my prince was ready to say goodbye.

Kanthaka, who was as sensitive a creature as any man, could not bear the thought of being parted from his master. Before my eyes, he breathed his last.

My sorrow doubled. Now I would have to return alone to the city. I would have to tell the king of his son's departure and suffer the punishment for having let him go. I did not regret what I had done.

I touched his feet and he blessed me. And then he walked away, into a mango grove, to meditate.

My prince gave up the earth, but in doing so, he won it. His long journey to Enlightenment began that night, but that was one journey he would have to make alone.

In her
**third
dream,**
the queen saw a
lion.

ou could call it the Puzzle of the Fourteen Dreams. Fourteen dreams that were dreamt by two women who had nothing in common except the dreams, and a mystical baby. One was a Brahmin lady. The other was a queen. And I was the one with the Key.

I am an interpreter of dreams. Every interpreter dreams of getting the chance I did. Because when two unconnected people have the same dream, you can be sure something extraordinary is about to happen. As you will see, something did.

The Brahmin lady's name was Devananda. She was expecting a child at the same time as Queen Trishala. One night, Devananda saw fourteen prophetic dreams that made her indescribably happy. After eighty-two days, in her luxurious palace so different from the Brahmin lady's modest home, Queen Trishala slept longer one night than usual. Her sleep was filled with images so real she could almost taste and hear and touch them. She did not know it, but she was dreaming the very same fourteen dreams that Devananda had seen. And neither did she know that that very night Devananda's child was transferred to her womb by the King of the Gods, Indra, and her child transferred to Devananda.

The next morning, the king summoned us to court.

'My wife, Queen Trishala, has had fourteen dreams,' he announced. 'I know they are auspicious and I sense they are prophetic. But what exactly, O learned men, do they prophesy for my son?'

And one by one, King Siddharth began recounting each dream, exactly as the queen had told him.

'In the first dream she saw an elephant,' the king began. 'No ordinary jungle elephant, but a tall and stately creature. It was whiter than an ocean of milk or a heap of pearls, whiter than the moon or the silver mountain. Wisdom shone from its eyes, which were as mild as its body was strong. It carried marks that no elephant has been seen with and instead of two tusks it had four! When it raised its trunk and trumpeted, the sound was like the thunder of a giant rain cloud. What do you understand from that, O learned men?'

We conferred among ourselves. As the chief interpreter, I had to speak.

'It means, O King, that your son will be exceptional,' I said. 'He will be physically strong but even stronger spiritually. He will endure a lot of hardship in his search for wisdom. The four tusks will be the four orders that he will establish.'

'Four orders? Do you mean religious orders or princely?' the king asked.

'Either, my lord, either.'

My heart was pounding. I felt that this was just the first of some incredible revelations.

'Well maybe the second dream will make it clearer,' King Siddharth said. 'Listen. In the second dream, the queen saw a bull. It was a majestic bull, whiter than the whitest lotus. Its face was noble, and its horns were perfectly curved and keenly pointed. Its down was fine and bright and soft. It pawed the earth and seemed afraid of no one.'

The meaning came to me at once. 'Your son, my lord, will be a leader and a teacher of men. He will have no flaws and fear no one.'

'Hmm,' said the king. 'It may make sense to you, but to me you talk in riddles. But let us proceed. In her third dream, Queen Trishala saw a lion. His mane was dazzling, whiter than a heap of pearls or a cluster of moonbeams. His head was large and round. His eyes were like flashes of lightning, the colour of red-hot molten gold, liquid and blazing. When he roared, she saw how sharp and white his teeth were. When he lashed his tail, she saw how long and tufted it was. And when he crouched to jump, she saw how perfect his claws were, and how powerful his limbs. And then, as she was admiring him, the lion jumped straight at her, entered her mouth and was gone.'

The court gasped. The third dream was even more spine-tingling than the first two. The courtiers were clearly at a loss. But not us.

'It is plain, my lord,' I said, my voice now tinged with the excitement of discovery. 'The child in Queen Trishala's womb will be a lion among men. His power will be immense and he will rule the world.'

The king smiled. Now that was more like it! A king's son, a king. Pleased, he rushed to recount the fourth dream.

'In the fourth dream, O learned men, Queen Trishala saw Lakshmi, the goddess of wealth. She was seated on a lotus, and around her neck she wore strings of milk-white pearls and leaf-green emeralds, and a garland of gold. But even more beautiful than all her ornaments was her face. Her eyes were large and pure as the water lily. It was hard to look at her, so brilliant was the light that surrounded her.'

Our answers were now flowing as fast as thought.

'Your son, my lord,' I said, 'is blessed by the goddess herself. He will enjoy great wealth and splendour. None will compare with him, his riches and his generosity will dazzle everyone.'

This, too, was to the king's liking. Generosity, like wealth, was a kingly trait. The dreams were proving to be even more auspicious than he thought!

'Well then, what do you make of the fifth dream,' he said, 'in which Queen Trishala saw a beautiful garland descending from the sky? It was woven of all the flowers that ever bloomed in all the seasons. Each flower was still fresh, not a single petal was crushed or drooping. Thousands of bees came humming towards the garland and the sound of the bees and the fragrance of the flowers was so strong that it filled the entire universe. What, O learned men, might this mean?'

'It tells of the sweetness of your son's world, my lord,' I said. 'His teachings will be so fresh, so new, so perfect for all times and so beautiful, that the entire universe will be touched by their sweetness and purity.'

'May it be so!' King Siddharth said. 'That seems good and proper. My son will wear a garland of greatness and make his old father proud! Now the sixth dream awaits your explanation. It was a full moon she saw as she slept. A full moon like a polished mirror, white as foam, white as a flamingo, white as the quiver of Cupid's arrows. It shone as if to remind all people of their absent loved ones. It flooded the earth with its luminous glow. So bright was it that the lilies floating on the water burst into full bloom, thinking that it was day!'

What a breathtaking dream! I hastened to reply. 'Peace, my lord. Your son will bring peace to the world. When the world sleeps, he will watch over all its hopes and dreams and help them to come to life.'

'Excellent!' the king exclaimed. Some of our excitement was now showing clearly on his face. 'For in her seventh dream, Queen Trishala saw the sun! Brighter than the flames of a raging forest fire, brighter than the moon and the stars put together, brighter than all the wealth in the world. The sun rose and the darkness fled. The demons and evil creatures that roamed the night shrivelled and died in the first rays of that thousand-rayed sun!'

'Yes, my lord, and so it will be with your son. He will bring the supreme knowledge that puts an end to the darkness of ignorance. He will destroy the dark thoughts and dark deeds of humanity, and everyone will be filled with the light of truth.'

Seven dreams had now been explained. There were seven more to go. As the king leaned back on his throne and exchanged a loving look with his queen, the court buzzed. The child to come seemed truly fortunate. All this in one child! The gods must have chosen him for a special purpose. The gods must have . . .

I felt strangely tired. Never before had I been called upon to interpret so many dreams at once. It was exhilarating but also exhausting. I had just closed my eyes when the king called out, 'Shall we continue?' The whispered discussions stopped. 'Seven more dreams!' the king said triumphantly. 'Seven more dreams to knowing my son's entire future!'

And so we continued.

The eighth dream was a flag on a golden staff. It fluttered in the breeze, so high that it seemed it would pierce the sky. Queen Trishala, who could not take her eyes from it, saw that it carried the emblem of a lion, white as crystal, as mother-of-pearl, white as a silver cup.

'Does this not mean dominion, O learned men?' the king asked us, for he was beginning to understand how we read the signs.

'Yes, my lord, it does,' I said. 'Your son will conquer many people, but not through wars. He will conquer through his teachings. The banner, my lord, that he will carry to far lands will be of faith.'

'So be it,' the king said, a trifle impatiently. 'But surely the golden vase in Queen Trishala's ninth dream indicates earthly glory? The queen says she has never seen such a splendid vessel before. Crafted out of the purest gold, and embedded with jewels, it was filled with the purest of water. The water was perfectly still, and the gold was reflected in its stillness.'

He looked at us expectantly. It was as if he was daring us to disagree with him! It often happens to us interpreters. People think what we do is easier than we admit.

'The meaning of this dream, my lord, is greater than what meets the eye,' I said, diplomatically. 'It means your son will be faultless, full of every virtue. His soul will be pure and brimming with compassion for every living creature, be it big or small, great or insignificant.'

'I see. And the lotus lake? That was Queen Trishala's tenth dream. Thousands of lotuses were floating on the lake. Water drops shone on their leaves like pearls. The queen marvelled at how many they were, and as she watched, the sun's rays fell on the lake and all the lotuses bloomed at once. Is my son the sun or the lotus? I am puzzled, O learned men, and more than a little tired.'

'Fear not, my lord,' I said. 'Your son is beyond both the lotus and the sun. He will not be tied down by worldly desires. He will be free, and in his freedom he will help liberate others from the cycle of birth, death and sorrow. From his calm, countless people will take comfort. Tell us, my lord, the eleventh dream.'

The eleventh dream was an ocean of milk, as turbulent as the lotus lake had been placid. The wind whipped the ocean, the tails of whales and porpoises lashed about on the surface, and the waves rose and rushed and roared. It bothered the king.

'Do you, O learned men, see trouble for my son?' he asked.

'No my lord,' I said. 'For your son will escape the turmoil that awaits all others. He will be infinitely wise and through his knowledge he will attain moksha.'

And so it went on. Each time the king saw earthly greatness, we saw spiritual greatness. The celestial abode of the twelfth dream could have meant both—glory on earth, and a place in heaven. It had a thousand and eight columns inlaid with gold and jewels and shimmering curtains of pearls. Pictures of wolves, bulls, horses, men, dolphins, birds, plants and fabulous beasts adorned it. It was illuminated with an invisible white light, and the gods themselves sang and beat the drums. But for us it meant only one thing. The king's son would be such a good spiritual master, that the gods themselves would bow down to him.

It was the same with the thirteenth dream, which was a heap of jewels, piled from the earth to the sky. King Siddharth saw grandeur and overflowing coffers, but we saw a treasure house of spiritual values, more precious than human understanding.

Till finally we reached the last and fourteenth dream and the king was in doubt no longer. Whatever destiny was to be his son's, one thing was certain. Either as an emperor or as a Tirthankara, King Siddharth's son would be second to none.

This is what the fourteenth dream revealed. In it, Queen Trishala saw a smokeless fire. Fed with honey-coloured ghee, the flames crackled and leapt, sparks flew, she felt the heat on her face, but she didn't see any smoke. Not a single curling wisp of grey rose into the sky, and yet the fire burned!

We were speechless at the wonder of this last and most prophetic sign.

'He will attain salvation, my lord,' I said, unable to hide the reverence in my voice. 'All his past lives will be behind him. He will destroy blind faith and replace it with seeing. He will remove meaningless rituals and replace them with learning. He will be a great prophet, a Tirthankara.'

I felt renewed. This was amazing news, and the closer we had come to this ultimate revelation, the harder it was to remain composed and grave, as a wise sage should be! No, right then, I felt as gleeful as a little child. But I had to play my part to the end. I bowed respectfully to the king and the queen, and then left the court. The other interpreters couldn't stop talking about the fourteen dreams, but I was content with the thought that I had helped to unlock their meaning.

From then on, I think I was more interested in palace events than in my work. It was as if that marathon dream-decoding had satisfied every instinct of mine as an interpreter. I recorded events and decoded omens instead. I saw good things everywhere. So did the entire kingdom. The whole period that Queen Trishala carried the blessed baby in her womb, King Siddharth's kingdom prospered. Riches, be they gold, silver, jewels, shells, precious stones or corals, multiplied. Crops grew lusher and greener. Armies grew larger, storehouses grew fuller, towns grew bigger, subjects felt happier and the glory of the kingdom was greater than it had ever been before. Seeing this, King Siddharth decided to call his son Vardhamana. He couldn't have chosen a better name, for it meant 'the increasing one'.

Now the child, who everyone knew by then was really a great soul, felt so much compassion for his mother who had grown big with him, that he decided to stay absolutely still. One day, when Queen Trishala realized that her baby was completely motionless, she felt afraid. 'What if something has happened to the child inside me? Or else, why does it not move?' This thought plunged her into sadness.

Soon, news of the queen's anguish spread throughout the palace. All the sounds of rejoicing—the drums, the pipes, the singing and clapping of hands, the acting of plays and the laughter of audiences—died. King Siddharth's palace became as silent as a tomb.

The child realized in his wisdom that he had unintentionally caused pain, and he moved.

Queen Trishala who was sobbing brokenly, suddenly felt a tiny movement inside her, and her tears changed to smiles. 'He is alive! My son is well, and alive! He moved! I felt it!' Saying this, she laughed gaily and the sound carried through the silent palace. Everyone, standing stock-still and sad, heard it.

Knowing all was well again, the merriment resumed. And so the child, who was destined to renunciation, decided that he would never leave his parents as long as they were alive, as that would bring them far more sorrow than they could bear.

After nine months, in the first month of summer, on the fourteenth day, when the moon shone clear, and the fields were green and beautiful, a baby boy was born to Queen Trishala at the stroke of midnight. Showers of petals fell from the heavens, and King Siddharth ordered ten days of festivities. The people celebrated with story-telling and ballad-singing, prisoners were pardoned and all debts were forgotten.

Prince Vardhamana was raised as any young prince would be in those days. He was cared for by five nurses, who loved him dearly and never tired of playing with him in a beautiful garden paved with precious stones. He learnt archery and horse-riding, philosophy and literature, the science of planning a military campaign and the science of running a kingdom. He took great interest in everything he was taught, for his mind was sharp and his skills instinctive. Everyone loved him for his endless energy and his persistent questioning, for Vardhamana had to know and do everything.

I never stopped observing the boy and so I noticed something else. The one thing that cannot be taught, he was born with. Courage.

Prince Vardhamana possessed courage far beyond his years. Soon his acts of bravery became legendary throughout the kingdom. There was the time a rogue elephant charged straight at him. Grown men fled out of the elephant's path, women shrieked, children wailed, but Vardhamana stood his ground. Before anyone could stop him, he raced towards the beast, clung to its trunk and climbed it. As he stood on the elephant's back it calmed down, and the amazed crowd cheered. Then there was the time Prince Vardhamana coolly picked up an enormous poisonous snake and flung it aside without coming to the slightest harm. Stories such as these gave Vardhamana a new name, one that his father himself would have approved. The name was Mahavira, which meant 'great conqueror'. It seemed King Siddharth's son would not be a Tirthankara after all!

I alone knew that destiny cannot be trifled with.

As all princes must do one day, Mahavira married a princess. Her name was Yasoda and they had a daughter named Anojja. King Siddharth and Queen Trishala couldn't have been happier. But when Mahavira was twenty-eight years old, the royal couple died. The kingdom went into mourning.

Mahavira, who had kept his word all these years, knew that at last the time had come for him to forsake the world. His elder brother Nandivardhana begged him to stay on, and so, to please him he agreed, but only if he was allowed to live like an ascetic. For two whole years, Mahavira lived in the palace only in name. He denied himself all the luxuries he had been used to, performed difficult penances and gave gifts and alms to countless beggars every day.

Finally, the two years were over. At the age of thirty, Mahavira renounced his wealth, his property, his family and his kingdom.

In a garden of the village Kundapura near Vaishali, he found a solitary Ashoka tree. There under the tree, facing east, he fasted for three days without drinking even a single drop of water, laid all his silken garments aside, tore the hair from his head in five strong handfuls and wrapped a single cloth around him. Then he made a vow that was as difficult as it was powerful.

'From this day on,' he vowed, 'for twelve whole years I will ignore my body and all its needs, and bear with complete calm all the hardships that heat and cold, rain and storm, people and animals may inflict on it.'

It was a mighty vow. I had followed Mahavira, unseen, to the garden. I wanted to inscribe in my memory the last worldly days of the boy whose birth I had in some way been part of. Something inside me wished to ask him for some final blessing. But I was too slow. A Brahmin beggar was passing by and seeing Mahavira, he asked for some alms. I knew Mahavira wouldn't turn away a Brahmin empty-handed. But what would he give him? He had cast away every single possession, every ornament, every piece of clothing right before my eyes. Suddenly, he unwrapped the single cloth that he wore and tearing it in half, handed it to the Brahmin. And then he walked on, to seek a life free from passion and desire, worry and strife.

I myself had foretold such an ending. I myself lived to see it come true, and learned more from his teachings than any dreams could have taught me. But somehow, at that moment, I felt as if something brand new had happened. Something so new and bright and good that it would be a long time before the magic wore off. It was like waking up in the morning, knowing that that day, and all the others that followed, would be glorious. And so indeed they were.

THE TEMPTER
& THE
HOLY MAN

'Crush him
like an insect!'
I ordered.

have been following Prince Siddhartha ever since the night he left home. My name is Mara. I am the Tempter, the Evil One, the One who Stalks like a Shadow and Pounces like a Beast. I have many names but only one aim. To sow doubt where there is faith and confusion where there is order. So far I have been remarkably successful.

At least, until this Prince Siddhartha came along. That night, I tried to make him go back to the ways of men. I knew he felt pain at the thought of leaving his pretty young wife and his newborn son. I felt his weakness call me like a cry for help and I rushed to him, but I could not make him stay. It had been a moment's weakness only. It passed, and the zeal and energy that is a young man's pride came back, and he ignored me. But I swore I would dog his every step till he fell, and here I am, seven years later, still trying. It has been a long seven years, for him, and for me. But at least I have the pleasure of knowing I am closer to my goal than I was then. Prince Siddhartha doesn't even have that!

Everyone else calls him the Bodhisattva. Everyone else but me. To me he will always be the lost Prince Siddhartha, wandering aimlessly those first few weeks, till he found those two teachers, Alara and Uddaka. Everyone said they knew about life and death and everything in between. Everyone, that is, but me. Naturally I did not intervene when Prince Siddhartha decided to become their disciple. The sooner he discovered his mistake the better for me!

And so the poor fool stayed there for a whole year, learning everything they had to tell him, and so in effect, learning nothing. At last, and not a moment too soon if you ask me, he gave up, took his leave, reverentially, and moved on till he came to the jungle of Uruvela. Deep in that treacherous jungle he found a band of five hermits.

The hermits were clearly out of their minds. They lived a life of extreme hardship. They ate only herbs and roots, slept on the cold hard ground, and spent hours on end meditating without moving or speaking or drinking a single drop of water! All this denial, for what? I could have granted them anything, if only they had yearned even once for a soft bed or a plate of succulent meat! But they didn't. They were as fixed on their goal as Prince Siddhartha, and as absorbed. The prince asked permission to join them and very soon he was outdoing them all. No torture was too much for him. No denial too great. Even I couldn't help feeling a sneaking respect for the lad when I saw what he was capable of. He could do great things in the world, with that kind of strength and intensity! If only I could tempt him back before he lost himself in that useless other-world . . .

How maddening it was to watch him these last six years! His flesh shrivelled till he became as thin as a dried-up branch. I amused myself by guessing when I would start seeing right through him! The less he ate, the more his reputation grew. People came from great distances to see the 'Muni of Extreme Asceticism'. But I knew my man better than anyone else. I could tell that Prince Siddhartha was unhappy. Whatever wisdom he was after was still as elusive as a butterfly in a field! I could see the struggle in his face as he forced himself to believe that this was the only way. But I restrained myself. My moment had not yet come.

For some days now all he had eaten was a single grain of rice each day. I knew why he did it. He hoped that by denying himself food, he would keep his mind clear and empty, a ready vessel for whatever light he hoped would pour into it like water. Ha! He was fooling himself.

To my great delight, one day I saw him keel over and collapse where he stood. Hunger had robbed him of all strength. For a moment I wondered if he were dead, for then I would have lost the battle without having begun it, and that would have made me mad. But no, he awoke and wonder of wonders, he ate some food!

I watched, gloating, but the hermits were outraged! How could he, who had outdone them all, give up now? The strongest had weakened first! Without giving him a chance to explain why, they walked away, rejecting him outright. Prince Siddhartha was alone again. He could have taken comfort in *my* presence at least, but he did not know I was always a step behind him, and I did not care to let him know.

Thin, wasted, deluded, he wandered on. And on. If I were not of unceasing energy myself, even I would have quailed. We had drawn close to the navel of the earth, out of which the great Bo tree grew. For once, he seemed to show no hesitation. He went straight up to the Bo tree and sat down under its branches.

Just then a woman appeared. I, who have the gift of knowing, knew it was Sujata, the daughter of a farmer. She had been coming to make an offering to the god of the Bo tree in thanksgiving for her newborn son. Seeing Prince Siddhartha seated under its mighty branches, the foolish woman assumed the god of the Bo tree had appeared before her. She bowed low and offered him the bowl of rice-milk. Prince Siddhartha, who had not seen such good food for six years, accepted it, and ate it all. Then, he closed his eyes and began to meditate.

A nasty prickling on my arms told me that the gods in their heavens were rejoicing. This was the moment they had all been waiting for. My patience dissolved into rage. It was *my* moment, and I would not let them take it away. I was seized by a malevolent glee.

'All this time I have clung to him like a shadow and never once has he weakened! But now, he is mine. For six years he has eaten what other men eat in a day! He is as feeble as a kitten and as helpless as a child. His mind, though he doesn't know it, hungers for distraction. Now at last, Prince Siddhartha, you will succumb to my wiles! Come, my daughters, let us break this man's foolish sense of purpose!'

And so saying, I, Mara, Lord of the Five Desires, Bringer of Death and Enemy of Truth, summoned my daughters to my side. They came at once, the three of them, Tanha, Raga and Arati, and along with them came a murderous army of evil demon-warriors.

I showed myself at last. On either side of me stood my daughters. Behind me, as far as the eye would go, stood my warriors. They remained hidden behind a magical mist of my making. I would not reveal all my cards at once! Besides, brute force was not enough to win Prince Siddhartha's mind. I would have to trick him. He wanted to save the world, didn't he? Well, I would use that against him now!

'Great sage!' I said, dripping honey into my words. 'How can you sit there so oblivious of the troubled world? You are weak and soon you will die for lack of food and water. What use will you be when you are dead? Have you ever thought of that? Give up this life of aimless wandering and useless contemplation and return to the real world! Many urgent tasks await you, O sage. Return to your family, your friends, your countrymen. They need you! Don't turn a deaf ear to their cries! If you are as good as everyone says, you would be helping them in their troubles, instead of sitting here, pleasing only yourself! Arise!'

It was, though I say so myself, fiendishly clever. My words were crafted to arouse guilt, or at least the first stirrings of doubt. I waited, still looking humble.

'I do not please only myself,' he said, at last. 'Ask the earth.' As he spoke he pressed the earth with his fingers and I heard a voice saying,

'It pleases me that my son has chosen this path. He has a right to sit here under this tree, in the fresh open air, and contemplate. Leave him alone!'

It was Mother Earth herself, speaking on his behalf. I seethed, I gnashed my teeth, but I had no option. I stepped away.

'No, he is too far gone for merely *lofty* things to stir him!' I said out loud. 'He needs something more appealing. Beware, Prince Siddhartha, for you are about to feel the stir of human desire!'

And in the flash of an eye, I took the shape of the Apparition of Lust and Vanity.

'Look, young prince,' I said. 'You are a young man, in the flush of youth. You should not be alone. You need company. I offer you my daughters in marriage. See how bewitching they are! Young, long-haired and lotus-eyed, they were made for a prince like you! Take them and rejoice in a world that is filled with beauty and love!'

And as I spoke, Tanha, Raga and Arati, my devilish young temptresses, danced before him as the dancing girls in his palace had once done, but he was blind to their charms.

'Fool of a man!' I yelled. 'What you are looking for will never please you as much as what I am offering you. You are insolent to think you can refuse Mara! You are asking for death! Death it shall be! Behold, Prince Siddhartha, the might of Mara!'

And I took the fearsome form of the Apparition of War and whisked away the mists that shielded my armies. A whirlwind arose out of nowhere. I threw darkness into the sky and whipped the roar of oceans into his ears. It was too much for even him to ignore. How could he, when I sat before him on my great war-elephant, urging rank upon rank of demon-soldiers to charge towards him, a tide of glittering weapons?

'Die!' I screamed and hurled my spear at him. He didn't move. Sitting where he was, he reached out his hand and touched the spear.

The spear turned into a lotus.

'You mock me!' I shrieked, unable to believe my eyes. 'Sorcery for sorcery!' And I hurled a thunderbolt at him, not one, but thousands, flung by my teeming warriors. He touched each one, and each one turned into a lotus and fell harmlessly to the ground.

I held myself back no more. Out of my empty hands I conjured up the reeking flames of hell, but before they could engulf him, they turned into perfumed breezes that made me choke and retch.

'Crush him like an insect!' I ordered, and led a charge that no man could ever hope to endure. All my armies fell on him at once. But before we could tear him apart, a golden cobra appeared out of the earth and shielded him from our blows with its hood. I hacked at the hood with my axe, my sword, and in utter fury, with my nails and my teeth, but it was no use. The man was protected from all harm.

I hate to say this, but I withdrew. I took my armies, and my daughters and my own defeated self, and vanished where I came from. All these years of waiting had been in vain. I would have cried tears of fury, had I been alone. The gods rained down a shower of flowers as I left. To me each flower stung like a serpent.

And so, now I'm here, back in the lower depths, waiting for easier prey. News gets to me of what goes on up there. I am told that after I left him, the prince went into meditation for forty-nine days. When he emerged he knew at last that ignorance is the source of all evil, and that right action, understanding, speech and effort would free all humans from suffering.

I am told that a god came down to test him, to play my role of the tempter! That must have been a laugh. Where I, the original Tempter had failed, how could anyone else succeed? I could have told them that! But nobody asked me and so the god in the guise of the tempter appeared before him and said, 'Wait O Buddha! You have learnt and seen what no man has before! Why don't you come with me to the land of gods then, instead of returning to the land of men?'

And Prince Siddhartha is supposed to have said, 'Because I must teach what I have learnt.'

The god laughed. 'Those you wish to teach are not willing to learn! How will you explain to them what has taken you so long to understand? And even if they understand it, they will not believe it! You are wasting your time!'

I must say he did well, the tempter god. Even I couldn't have put it better. But as I could have guessed, the words had no impact. Prince Siddhartha replied, 'Even if one person hears and learns, it is enough for me!' And smiling, he went back to his homeland to fulfil his strange destiny. It wasn't one I would have chosen for him.

And so now everyone calls him the Buddha. Everyone that is but me. For me he will always be Prince Siddhartha, the one who lost his way, the one who defeated Mara, the one who would not, who could not be tempted.

I wanted to

push him off

the tower...

t the time when Jesus was still living quietly as a carpenter in the city of Nazareth, news of an electrifying preacher spread through Judea like wildfire.

'There is this man,' they said, 'who has come out of the desert—his hair is matted with sand and his clothes are the colour of stone. For years he has wandered alone, up and down the desolate shores of the Dead Sea. He has eaten nothing but locusts and wild honey, and he has slept under the cold shine of the stars. But when he speaks! It is like fire struck out of flint! It is like lightning ripping open the sky! They call him John the Baptist and they say he has a message for us all. He is baptizing anyone who will come to repent in the waters of the Jordan. Come with us, for we are headed that way!'

And so groups of people from all over Israel rushed to see John the Baptist and hear what he had to tell.

'The Messiah is coming!' John the Baptist declared. 'The greatest of them all! But you are unprepared, all you people! You are sinful and wicked. Repent and you may still find room in your hearts for him when he comes!'

Some of the people who came felt afraid when they heard these fiery words. It seemed more like a warning than a revelation. What were they to do? Out of a mixture of timidity, hope and fear they allowed John the Baptist to plunge their heads into the water and declare them cleansed. Pitiful people! They just wanted to be on the safe side for the Messiah when he came, *if* he came. The others, who had rushed to the spot hoping for some grand spectacle, felt let down and went back, cursing themselves for having made the trip at all.

'Are you not the Messiah yourself?' the disappointed ones asked John the Baptist, for his presence was magnetic and his words full of power.

'I am not!' cried John. 'He who will come will be far mightier than I. I am not even fit to tie the thongs of his sandals! All I am doing is preparing his way, making the crooked straight and the rough smooth! I baptize with water, but he will baptize you with fire and the Holy Spirit!'

Such words only left the people dissatisfied and restless to know more. I knew exactly how they felt. I myself had been waiting thirty long years for Jesus to make his appearance. All this time he had not made a single rousing speech or performed a single miracle that would have given me a chance to destroy him. Impatience and irritation were my constant companions all this tedious time.

But now, as if roused out of a stupor, he approached the banks of the river Jordan at last and only I and the wild-haired preacher recognized him. He waited his turn meekly. I watched, invisible.

When he stepped up to John the Baptist, the older man said, 'I cannot baptize you! I am not worthy enough.'

But Jesus insisted he do so. And so, John the Baptist, whose voice was harsh with preaching and whose hands were gnarled with age, baptized Jesus. Jesus stood with the waters of the Jordan waist-high around him, praying, when a dove fluttered out of the sky and settled on his shoulder. The mere sight of it filled me with pain. And then a great voice came out of the sky and said, 'You are my beloved son!'

It was done. Jesus had been proclaimed the Messiah and now I could act. As if to make my task easier, he left the banks of the Jordan and wandered as far as he could from the teeming multitudes by the river.

I knew how he felt. He, too, had been preparing for this moment all his life. Now it was upon him. Like me, he felt elated and overwhelmed, but unlike me, he felt afraid, because he was a man.

He walked as if blind, paying no attention to where his feet led him. Stumbling over hard rock, drifting over plain and dune he wandered, lost in his thoughts and the enormity of what lay ahead. It was as if time itself had become meaningless for him and the physical world a mirage. He seemed to forget he was made of flesh, for he forgot hunger, thirst and pain. The sun scorched his bare hands and face but he made no effort to shield himself. Stones cut his feet and bruised his body when he slept, but he made no effort to move. Sand blew into his eyes and hair and mouth.

We walked, he and I, locked in a tumultuous silence. He spoke to no one because no one walked in that wilderness. For forty days, he walked, alone except for me, in that inhospitable wilderness, and at the end of forty days he could hardly stand. I knew how he felt—

light-headed, tired to the bone and hungry like he had never been before. But where would he find food? He was still far from the edge of the city. Not even a cactus grew anywhere.

And then he heard my voice.

'Why do you faint with hunger?' I said in my softest, sweetest voice. 'Surely *god* would not want his own son to die of such a *miserable* thing as hunger, when he has such an *important* mission to complete! Or could it be, that you are not his son after all? That makes sense! No wonder you weaken and swoon like any ordinary mortal!'

Jesus did not answer.

'Do I take your silence to mean defeat then?' I said, relentless as a whip. 'Show me you are not defeated! If you are the son of god himself, then prove it to me. There is no bread in the desert but there are plenty of stones lying at your feet. Pick one up and turn it into a loaf of bread, so that I may know for certain who you are!'

I have seen hunger drive men to murder. It is a powerful weapon, hunger, and in my hands it was a double-edged sword. A single crust of bread was all it would take for Jesus to hush both the growl in his belly and the soft voice at his ear. In one stroke he would prove his greatness, and betray it. It was a wonderful trap. He would succumb. He had to!

I was mistaken.

'You are mistaken,' he said, his voice cracked from disuse, but firm. 'Man does not live by bread alone. My God will sustain me in other ways, ways that will always be a mystery to you. I know what you are trying, but it is of no use, so go away and leave me alone.'

How could I! Not after all this time. I would wait. I had waited thirty years and forty days, what were a few hours more? I followed him as he walked on and climbed a high mountain near Jerusalem. Wandering around in the parched flatlands, he had lost all sense of direction. I could have shown him the way, if only he had trusted me. But no, he preferred to climb to the top of the mountain from where he would get a perfect view of which way his city lay. I stood by his elbow and saw what he saw. All the lands of Judea stretched before us, shimmering in the sunlit haze.

'It is a glorious sight is it not?' I whispered into his ear. 'Look!' And with a wave of my hand I rolled away the haze so that Jesus saw lying before him in perfect and bewitching clarity not only the kingdom of Israel but all the kingdoms of earth, revealed by me in an instant.

I could see he was impressed. He caught his breath. I rushed into the breach.

'You marvel, do you not!' I gloated, gently. 'This is just the beginning. Such is my power that I can reveal to you things you have not seen or dreamt of! All those lands you see are mine and I alone can give them to you. You can be king! Emperor! All the domains of the earth can be under your sway! In an instant! All you have to do in return is bow down and worship me, me!'

I was carried away. It was all that pent-up impatience, bursting out like a flood. He would be swept off his feet by my eloquence! He would . . .

'Never! I will never bow down to you!' His voice cut into my thoughts like a thorn. I winced. He continued, relentless. 'I serve only one God, and it is to Him that I bow down! These earthly kingdoms mean nothing to me.'

What certainty! What arrogance! Speechless at his resistance, I could do only one thing. I followed him as he left the barren, rocky desert and walked into Jerusalem.

Entering the city, he went at once to the temple. I shuddered but I entered it too. He walked right up to the pinnacle. I walked behind him. He was weary and he stumbled. 'Beloved city, how I long to rest my eyes on you again!' he muttered to himself as we climbed. Homecoming had made him sentimental. He was weak again. That suited me.

We reached the top. He breathed the air deeply, and then he realized he was not alone.

'Your trust in your god is touching!' I sneered. 'You reject food for his sake, you reject great wealth and importance for his sake, now why don't we see if *he* will do something for *your* sake?'

The temple of Jerusalem was a mighty temple, at least in the eyes of men. It towered into the sky and up on the pinnacle where we stood, a strong breeze blew, tugging at Jesus' robes. One wrong step and it would be a long fall to the ground below. I laughed at the thought and began nudging Jesus closer and closer to the edge, talking all the while in my subtle and provocative way.

'You see the drop, don't you?' I said. 'A mortal man will not survive it. But one such as yourself, who claims to be the son of god—why, for you, it should not be deadly! Hasn't your father said that he will send his angels to lift you up and carry you away so that you do not hurt yourself against the stones? Well then, why are you afraid? Why do you hesitate? Throw yourself off this tower and prove to me that your god loves you as much as you love him!'

We teetered dangerously at the edge. I saw him look down. He looked pale and proud. Perhaps at last he would dare to take up my challenge. I had accused his god of not loving him enough. He would not be able to take it. That too from me. I smiled.

Perhaps that was what made him change his mind. He stepped back and looked at me, with something horrifyingly like pity in his eyes.

'You forget, Satan,' he said. 'You forget that He has also said that no one shall put Him to the test! Not even me. No taunt of yours will make me betray His trust. The proof of His love is in my heart, and that is why it hurts you, for you have no heart, just darkness and a terrible pain.'

I wanted to push him off the tower when he said that. I wanted to watch him die, painfully. I wanted to tear out the dusty hair that the wind tossed about his face and shred his robes to pieces with my nails. I wanted to ruin him. But I could not. Instead, I stood there a long time, watching him. I stood there till he took a deep breath and began the long climb down.

THE
REVELATION

'Recite!'

the invisible being
commanded.

veryone knew Abd al-Muttalib's sons. They were the handsomest men in Mecca. When they walked through the streets, men exclaimed and women blushed. But the handsomest one among them was Abdullah. He was the youngest and he was blessed with the bearing of a prince! There wasn't a single one among us girls who didn't dream of him in secret. But what chance did we have? Abd al-Muttalib was one of the wealthiest and most important men in the city. His father Hashim used to send two richly laden caravans to Syria and Yemen every year. I remember my grandfather telling me how even the emperors of Byzantium and Abyssinia always had time and a good word for the founder of the Hashim clan. My clan was the Zurah and we were not as powerful as the Hashim, leave alone the Quraysh who were then the most powerful tribe in the whole of Arabia. So for me, dreams of marrying Abd al-Muttalib's youngest son were no more than just that—dreams.

And then, one day, the news flew from house to house—Abd al-Muttalib is looking for a bride for Abdullah! My heart lurched. I had been dreading this day and yet now that it had come, I was seized by an irrational hope.

'Abd al-Muttalib is looking outside his clan! The Hashim clan is not what it used to be.' 'Their fortunes are declining. They need to make a profitable match.' 'There is a chance for our daughters!'

Scraps of excited gossip reached my ears. My cousins began spending hours before the mirror and their mothers spent hours at the bazaar, buying silk and lace and sweetmeats. Everyone was in a ferment. Who would Abd al-Muttalib choose for his youngest son?

It was like something out of those fairy tales we used to love as children. He chose me.

Me, Amina bint Wahb, who hadn't a chance in all the world. An uncle of mine arranged it. He was a leading merchant of Zurah and he made the proposal. Here was a perfect combination. A beautiful girl. A good family. A profitable alliance. And next thing I knew, I was being wedded to Abdullah, prince among men, the secret love of my life!

My cousins refused to speak to me. Some of them shut themselves up in their rooms, and refused to come out, saying their hearts were totally and utterly broken. I was too delirious to care. I was waiting for my new husband to come home.

I waited for what seemed like a long time. Finally, he came, and on his face there was mischief mixed with love.

'You're lucky I'm here!' he laughed. 'A strange and beautiful woman almost didn't let me come!'

I sulked and pouted and wept. What beautiful woman? How could he? And then he consoled me and said, 'No, my little bird, I was walking through the marketplace when this woman threw herself at my feet and begged me to take her home for just one night. "Don't you know I have just got married," I told her. "Find yourself another man, sister," I said, and walked away. Aren't you proud of me?'

'No,' I sulked. 'You made me wait and that is unforgivable!'

And then of course we made up. It was only later that I realized why that strange woman had thrown herself at my husband's feet. Right then, I was too lost in watching my dream unfold into reality. Abdullah was sweeter, funnier, gentler than any prince could be, and I was mad with joy. Before long, I was carrying his baby and our house was filled with rejoicing.

It was too good to last. One morning, without warning, Abdullah died. The world went dark before my eyes. In one stroke, all that had been bright and good had been snatched away. More misfortune awaited me. It turned out Abdullah had left nothing but five camels and a slave girl to me. That was all that remained of his family's wealth. How was I to live? How was I to bring up my little baby?

It was the thought of my baby that brought me back to life. The sadness eased as I felt the baby move. I felt no discomfort, the way other mothers-to-be around me complained. Instead, I felt calm and weightless.

One day, as I sat quietly by myself, I sensed a radiant light streaming from my belly. It shimmered in front of me and in it, as I would in a crystal ball, I saw the faraway castles of Syria. It was near enough to touch and yet it was impossibly far away. As I sat and wondered, a great voice spoke and said, 'Your son, Amina, wife of Abdullah, will be the lord of all Arabia!'

I looked around. Who had spoken? But I could see nothing except that heavenly light, and soon it faded and I was left alone with the memory of its beauty and the power of that wonderful voice.

It was then that I understood that strange woman in the marketplace. She must have seen a light in Abdullah's eyes that told her he would be the father of the Great One. She would have done anything to be the woman who brought God's messenger into the world. Poor creature! That was not to be her fate.

On the twelfth of Rabi'u al-awwah, my son Muhammad was born. It was a day of great thanksgiving. Abd al-Muttalib came and fell to his knees when he saw his grandson. He had heard of my vision, and it was just as a *kahin* or soothsayer had prophesied. One of his descendants, the *kahin* had told him, would rule the world. And soon after that he had dreamt of a child from whose back a great tree arose. Its top touched the sky and its branches reached east and west. An intense light shone out of the tree and all of Arabia fell down and worshipped the light.

My son, Muhammad, was to be that light. Contented, I fell asleep with my baby held tightly to me.

. . .

Once, the Quraysh had been like us. Nomads, rough and ready, always on the move, not sure of the next meal, sometimes desperate, but never unhappy. Now, the Quraysh had grown fat. They lived in the city and made money. Bankers, merchants, moneylenders, they had forgotten the ways of the desert. But one thing they hadn't forgotten. The desert made children grow strong and sturdy. In the city, children grew up spoilt and sickly, pampered by useless luxuries. That was why they came to us, the Bedouins.

We Bedouin women looked after the rich Qurayshi children. They roamed about with our own and grew dark as dates and tall as palms. We liked having them with us. We also needed the money their parents paid us, for times when trade was poor and elders were ill. It was an old arrangement and a good one. But that year was bad. Even the Quraysh had suffered losses from famine and drought. There was a rush to take care of those children whose families had some money left to offer.

By the time I reached Mecca, I was dying of fatigue, and already late. The donkey I rode on dragged its feet and almost fell down. I got off, my own newborn at my breast crying for the milk that I could not give him. My she-camel was so thin and feeble it had stopped giving milk altogether. We were desperate.

'All the richer children are taken,' my husband informed me, his face grim with tiredness. 'There is only Amina's son, Muhammad. Will you take him?'

I was too tired to say no. Even if Amina gave us only a few coins, we could buy milk for my child. I nodded.

The boy they handed me was lovely. Even in my heart-sore, faintlimbed state, I felt a gush of pride as I held him to me. And then, a miracle happened. My milk flowed again and there was enough for Amina's son and my own! Blissfully well fed, the two boys fell asleep at once. My husband and I looked at each other, not daring to utter what we hoped.

'I will go and see,' my husband said after a while.

He came back running, in his hand an overflowing pail. 'Look Halima!' he exclaimed. 'I have milked our camel! And there's still more! You have taken a blessed child!'

And so it seemed I had. After weeks, we slept undisturbed by the rumblings of hunger.

Next morning, we set out from Mecca for our own home. We were a big group. I sat on my faithful donkey, Muhammad in my arms, my own son strapped to my back. I hoped the poor beast would not collapse on the long trudge home.

I needn't have worried! No sign remained of the previous day's exhausted animal! It trotted along briskly, and before long I left my companions far behind me.

'Wait for us!' they called out. 'No need to show off your new donkey!'

'What new donkey?' I called back. 'This is the same old one I came on!'

'Then either you are fooling us, or it is a miracle!' they said.

'What do you think!' I answered gaily, and trotted off once again.

We reached Bani Sa'd at last, where my home is. Always a bleak and barren land, that year it was wretched. The land stretched dry and yellow. But right in the middle there was an unbelievable patch of green. We hurried forward. It was the pasture in front of my house!

'What have you done, Halima?' my envious neighbours asked me. 'Your camels are thriving while ours are running dry. Not a shred of grass on our land and look at yours—a garden!'

'Send your camels to graze with mine then!' I said. They did so, but it was of no use. Their camels stayed dry. It seemed I was chosen to be the lucky one that year. My children had never had so much to eat. My husband had never been happier. And as for me, my heart overflowed each time I looked at Muhammad playing with my sons. He was such a good boy and my children loved him so! I dreaded the moment Amina would ask me to send Muhammad back to her. I would miss him, not just because of the good fortune he had brought us, but because he felt so close to me.

The first time Amina sent word for Muhammad, I begged to be allowed to keep him just a bit longer. Amina, bless her kind heart, agreed, and I began harbouring the hope of watching him bloom into a man.

But one day, something happened that changed my mind.

I was at home, cooking the midday meal, when my two elder

boys rushed in screaming. 'Ammi! Come quick! Two strange men in white have captured Muhammad and cut open his belly!'

I went cold. I rushed out, and there he lay, sprawled against the winter snow. As I shook him by the shoulders, he stirred, dazed and weak. I couldn't see a wound. Thank God! Gathering him up in my arms, I carried him into the warmth of the kitchen.

'What happened, son?' I whispered.

'I don't remember,' he said, and fainted.

Later, after he had had a bowl of soup and a piece of hot bread, he told me what had happened. Two men dressed in white had come up to him as he was playing. Though they were strangers he was not frightened. 'Come,' they said, and gently they took out his heart from his body and washed it in a patch of pure white snow. Strangely, he felt no pain. Then, they put his heart back, and lifted him on to a pair of scales. 'You are heavier than all the rest of the Arabs put together,' they said. Then one of them bent forward, kissed him on the forehead and said, 'Never be afraid, for you are the beloved of God. If you knew what He has planned for you, you would be filled with unutterable joy.' And then the two men had vanished and Halima had lifted him into her arms and he had fainted.

I couldn't understand what all this meant. Was Muhammad suffering from some strange illness? What if it happened again? What if the poor child died? What answer would I give to Amina then, who had entrusted her son to me? No, though it saddened me to even think it, Muhammad would be better off with his mother. And so, with heavy hearts, my husband and I decided to take him back to Mecca. My children sobbed and clung to Muhammad, refusing to let him go.

When we told Amina the whole story, we were a bit afraid of what she might say. But to our surprise, she was not alarmed.

'It is a sign, dear sister,' she said to me, her face beaming with pride. 'A sign of my son's greatness. Listen,' and she told us of the vision she had seen and the voice she had heard and of Abd al-Muttalib's dream about the boy.

I trembled when I heard. Amina thanked us for looking after him all these years, and pressed food and gifts into our hands before we left, but I could hardly even thank her properly. My mind was dizzy. I had been blessed even more than I could imagine. The Prophet himself in my care!

Taking one long last look at Muhammad, I left, weeping bitterly. Muhammad wept too, for he loved us, but I knew he would recover in time. Children always do.

Bani Sa'd seemed empty without him. Whenever anyone went to Mecca, I sent small gifts for him, a toy crafted by my son or a handful of dates. He was well and happy, they told me when they returned. I missed him dearly but was glad he was thriving.

And then one day, I heard bitter news. Amina had died.

Muhammad was just six years old. It seemed the poor child was destined to be orphaned over and over again. I would have rushed to him, but I knew I couldn't. My part in his story was over.

. . .

I had heard of Abu Talib's nephew. Orphaned child of Abdullah and Amina, beloved grandson of the aging Abd al-Muttalib, the young man everyone called al-Amin, the reliable one. Misfortune seemed to have shadowed that boy, he never saw his father, his mother died when he was six, and his grandfather when he was eight. He must have been lonely and sad.

Luckily for him, Abu Talib was a good man. Not that he was as wealthy as the chiefs of Hashim had once been, but he had a big heart. He took Muhammad in with open arms, and trained him in the trade. One of my men was then working with Abu Talib. He came back with a curious tale.

It took place on Muhammad's first trip with his uncle to Syria. When they reached Basra, the local monk, a man by the name of Bahira, rushed out of his tent and invited Abu Talib and his men to share a meal with him. Abu Talib was surprised. Bahira was a recluse, and on all the occasions they had passed his tent before, he had never once invited them in, let alone come out to meet them! Happy to have a chance to rest their tired feet, they gladly accepted. Muhammad, being the youngest, was told to guard the merchandise while they ate.

Inside the tent, Bahira examined the men closely. 'Is any one of your company missing?' he said, after a while.

At this, Abu Talib was a bit embarrassed. It was not proper to have left Muhammad, the grandson of the venerable Abd al-Muttalib, outside as if he were a servant. He called him in to join them.

The monk watched Muhammad carefully, but said nothing. When the meal was over, he took him aside.

'I am interested in knowing about your life, my child,' he said. 'Swear by the goddesses al-Lat and al-Uzza that you will answer my questions truthfully.'

'Do not ask me to swear by the goddesses,' Muhammad replied. 'I will swear by Allah alone.'

Hearing this answer, Bahira asked Muhammad to remove his shirt and turn around. Right there, between his shoulder blades, was the mark of prophecy!

'Abu Talib!' he said, excitedly. 'I must confess I did not invite you on a mere impulse. When I looked out of my tent today, I saw a bright cloud moving above your caravan. That is the sign of the Prophet's coming! This young boy's wise answer and the mark on his back have proved it. Take your nephew back home safely at once. If people know what I know, they will do him great harm! A great future is his, make sure he lives to fulfil it!'

The story made me think. How much of it was true and how much my man had made up to seem important in my eyes, I couldn't tell. But still, my curiosity was aroused. Everyone told me good things about Muhammad. How honest his gaze was, and how firm his handshake. How capable and trustworthy he was in matters of business, and how skilled in wrestling and sport. He was a quiet man, they told me. He knew how to listen. He had inherited his father's good looks and his mother's gentle ways. He had started leading caravans to Mesopotamia and Syria on his own. I decided I had to meet him.

'Tell Muhammad that Khadija bint Khuwaylid would like to give him an assignment. It is an important assignment and I am afraid to entrust it to anyone but him who is called al-Amin, the reliable one.'

My messenger came back with a positive reply. I was delighted. Within a few days they had left carrying merchandise to Syria. When they returned, my man had news to share.

'There is more to al-Amin than we know,' he said, mysteriously. 'Wherever I went, I was told remarkable things. A monk called me aside and said Muhammad is the prophet that all of Arabia has long been waiting for. Later, I saw with my own eyes two angels protecting Muhammad from the blazing sun!'

So there was more to it than mere rumour, I thought to myself. I asked my cousin who studied the Scriptures if what people were saying was true.

'It is indeed,' my cousin replied. 'Muhammad is to be our Prophet!'

I had known for some time that Muhammad was looking for a

wife. Made bold by some inner prompting, I asked him to marry me. I do not know what made him accept. True, I was one of Mecca's most successful women merchants, but he was destined for far greater things. But accept he did, and my life for the next ten years was filled with the laughter and games of our four daughters and our two little sons.

Muhammad was a pillar of support, not just to me and my family, but the clans as well. Success had set one clan against another in Mecca. Nothing could be solved without a dispute. Not even something as sacred as the work on the Kaaba. Our most sacred shrine had just been repaired, and the Black Stone had to be replaced in the eastern corner, just the way it had always been for centuries. But which clan would have the privilege of putting it back? A great quarrel arose. For five days they argued without reaching any decision. Finally one day they decided they would ask the first person who came by and do whatever he said.

They were lucky. That person happened to be my husband.

'Just the person we need!' the clansmen said. 'Who better than al-Amin to settle this quarrel!'

Muhammad heard them out and then asked for a white cloak. Puzzled, they got him one.

'Place the Black Stone in the middle of the cloak,' he said. They did so.

'Now each clan choose a representative and let him step forward.'

The representatives stepped forward.

'Now hold the cloak and lift it all together, and each clan will have had a hand in putting the Black Stone back where it belongs!'

It was the kind of simple solution only he could have come up with. Everyone was happy, but none more than me.

Our years together passed peacefully. However, things in Mecca were beginning to trouble Muhammad. Wherever he looked, he saw greed for money and power. He began withdrawing to the hills to meditate.

One day, he had a revelation. I will never forget that day, or how he looked when he came rushing home, quivering like a leaf and pale with fear and awe.

It was the seventeenth day of Ramadan, in the year 610. He was standing on the top of a mountain outside Mecca when it happened. Suddenly, without warning, he found himself held in the crushing embrace of an invisible being.

'Recite!' the invisible being commanded.

His breath was being squeezed out of him. Muhammad was afraid. 'I cannot recite,' he said, despairingly. 'I am not a *kahin*. Let me go!'

But the invisible being held him tighter and said, 'Recite!'

And without knowing how, my husband found himself speaking. The words poured out of him, what were to be the very first words of the Quran.

He couldn't tell when the invisible being released him, but when he came to his senses, he found himself lying outside the cave on the top of the mountain, drained. Who had visited him? What were the words he had spoken? Who had spoken the words through him? Terrified and feeling terribly alone, he jumped to his feet and started running down the mountain. Halfway down, he heard a voice saying, 'Stop O Muhammad! You are the apostle of God and I am the angel Gabriel!'

The voice was not louder than a whisper, but it filled the skies and echoed along the mountain walls. He turned to see who had spoken and saw the angel Gabriel in the shape of a man, standing with his feet spanning the whole horizon. The sight was so imposing that it rooted him to the spot. He turned his face away and shook his head, as if to prove he wasn't dreaming, but wherever he looked, Gabriel was there, immense and terrifying and kind.

God had revealed Himself to Muhammad.

When he told me this, I embraced him and rejoiced. My Muhammad had found his calling. He had been chosen to be God's messenger to the Arabic people. And I had been chosen to be his companion through it all.

God's word was hard to understand and even harder to express. Every time a new revelation came to him, he would tremble as if he were a bell being rung. I would look and be afraid for him. But then each time he would see the meaning, and when he explained it to me, I would feel as if I had walked into the brightest dawn of all.

If I lived

a million
years
on air alone...

saw it before anyone else. The rest were too busy looking into his face and saying things like, doesn't he have his father's handsome nose? And isn't his complexion just like his mother's—all milk and rose petals? And isn't it a glorious day that Mehta Kalu should have got a son at last? There was so much excitement and so many different types of sweets to eat that nobody had time to see what really mattered. That my little brother was born for greatness.

If anyone really looked, they would have seen the hidden light that played in his baby features. It shone and seemed to have some secret message for me alone, only I was too young to tell what it meant. All I knew then was that my brother was special. Maybe all sisters feel that way about their little brothers. What did I know? For me, just seeing little Nanak's face was enough to make me want to dance round and round and sing.

We were inseparable. Little Nanak is Bibi Nanki's little shadow, my mother's friends would tease each time the two of us came home after playing. What fun we used to have! We'd make boats out of leaves and sail them down the river, Nanak urging his boat to win and crying when it sank instead, too fragile for the strong current. To cheer him up, I'd make kites and we'd fly them. How we ran, and how the wind tugged at our kites, impatient to tear them loose! On some days all we did was race through the yellow mustard fields, stopping only to ask a kind neighbour for a stick of sugar cane, which we'd share, tearing at it with our teeth till the clear sweet juice rushed into our throats. And then, wildly hungry after all that running around in the fresh sun-drenched air of my village, we'd run home for my mother's soft rotis and a glass of fresh cool milk. Nothing compares to the kind of life we used to have those days as children in the Punjab. But like all good things, those carefree days too came to an end, and it was time for Nanak to go to school.

No more roaming about and playing with girls, my father had decided. Time for Nanak to learn to read and write, and who knows, if he proved to be good with numbers, study to be an accountant just like him.

And so, at the age of seven, my poor little Nanak found himself sitting inside a classroom, watching the teacher write the alphabet on the board. I can see his face scrunching up with concentration as he watched the teacher's patient hand outline each of the letters in chalk. The other children were missing their mothers or pulling each other's hair or finding other ways of not paying attention. Not my Nanak. He put up his hand.

Pandit Gopal Das, who was as good a man as there could be, looked a bit surprised. Children of Nanak's age rarely asked questions on the first day.

'What is it, Nanak?' he asked.

'Please sir, it's about the meaning of each of the letters you've written,' my brother said.

The meaning of each of the letters? I can see Pandit Gopal Das suppressing a smile.

'No, child, each of the letters alone has no meaning,' he said. 'It's when you put them together to form words that they start making sense—like the word b-a-l-l, ball, which you play with, and s-u-n, sun, which shines in the sky.'

I can see Nanak listening intently. Pandit Gopal Das was about to resume his lesson, when he noticed a little hand up in the air again. Nanak.

'Yes?' he asked.

'I can tell you sir, if you let me,' my brother said. 'I know the meaning of each of these letters!'

And before his teacher could say a word, Nanak began to speak. The other boys stopped crying and fidgeting and fighting. They were amazed that one of *them* should be teaching their teacher! They watched with open mouths. As for Pandit Gopal Das, he was dumbstruck. Was this boy just seven? Impossible! He was demonstrating how each of the letters of the alphabet was really a manifestation of God! No one could have taught him that. It had to be the divine spirit talking through the boy! He was deeply moved, and also humbled by the limitations of what he knew, with all his years of experience. Pandit Gopal Das dismissed the class for the day and decided to walk Nanak home, thus becoming the second person after me to realize that my brother was no ordinary boy.

My father however, was not happy to see his son coming home early on the very first day of school, that too accompanied by his teacher. He must have done something wrong. Whatever it was, he would make sure the boy was punished. Disobedience was not to be tolerated!

No one could be stricter than my father!

Fearing that Nanak would get a thrashing, I rushed behind my father as he hurried out to meet them.

'What has he done, Panditji?' my father asked. 'I'm sorry if he has caused you any trouble, and I promise it will not happen again!'

Panditji smiled.

'No no, Mehtaji,' he said. 'I haven't come to complain. Your son is a gem, one in a million. I do not think I can teach him anything he does not know. In one morning Mehtaji, he has taught me more than I learnt in a lifetime! He is an extraordinary boy, your Nanak. I think he is destined for great things. Look after him well, Mehtaji, and one day he will teach us all!'

I beamed. Panditji had put into words what I had only felt in my heart. I caught Nanak's hand and squeezed it.

'Isn't it too soon to tell, Panditji,' my father said, not looking too pleased. He would have been happier if his son had been an ordinary boy who followed in his footsteps like an ordinary dutiful son. What was all this talk of great things? It made him uncomfortable, I could tell. But my father respected Pandit Gopal Das and so he decided to listen to him. 'Since you say so, let him be. I hope things turn out all right!'

From that day on, my little brother was a free bird. It was like being children together again. But something had changed. He wasn't my shadow any more. No, he wandered off on his own all the time. Besides, I was a big girl by then. I had so many things to do about the house, pounding the spices, drying the pickles, washing my beautiful black hair, chatting with my girlfriends. Also, after what Panditji had said, I had begun to feel a little in awe of Nanak. I know, it sounds strange. But suddenly he was not just my brother. He was the brother who would become a saint. I had always known that but now it was out in the open, and it made me treat him differently.

Not so my father. Papaji was determined to treat his son just like any other boy his age. So he arranged for all the usual customs to be carried out, each at the right and proper time. When Nanak turned nine, we prepared for the sacred thread ceremony. The entire village was invited. The family priest began chanting the mantras. Everything was going well, until the priest bent over to put the thread around Nanak's neck.

'I refuse to wear it,' he said.

The entire gathering was scandalized. What an inauspicious thing to do! I could see my father frowning. My uncles felt maybe the boy hadn't understood the meaning of the ceremony. 'Explain it to him,' they said.

Elders explained. The priest quoted some texts. But Nanak had made up his mind. He heard them out, and then he said, 'What is the use of wearing a sacred thread if one's acts are unholy? This thread is made of cotton. Once it breaks what will I do? Throw it away and wear another one. What is the use of a thread that is not strong enough to last a lifetime?'

He may not have known it, but this was to become the first of his many important teachings. The priest, however, felt peeved. What absurd questions the boy asked!

'What kind of sacred thread would *you* like to wear then?' he asked.

'A thread of contentment, spun out of the cotton of kindness,' my brother answered at once. 'A thread knotted by moderation and made strong by truth. A thread, O priest, for my soul, that will never be soiled, or lost, or broken!'

Who could find fault with such beautiful words! The priest had no option but to let Nanak have his way.

My father, as you can imagine, was most upset. 'First the boy doesn't go to school, next he refuses the sacred thread!' To keep him out of any further mischief, Papaji gave him a list of chores to do. One of them was to take the buffaloes owned by our family to graze in the pasture.

One day, while he was in the field, Nanak fell fast asleep. With no one to keep an eye on them, our buffaloes walked into the neighbouring field, trampled the grass and nibbled away at the crops. When the owner saw what had happened, he was furious. He ran to Rai Bular, the officer in charge of our area and lodged a complaint against Nanak. Rai Bular called Papaji and Nanak to his office. My father was shaking with anger. Not because he had been summoned, but because his son could obviously do nothing right.

My brother, however, was unruffled. 'Go see for yourself, Rai Bular,' he said. 'The neighbour's crops are not destroyed at all!'

My father must have thought his son had started lying as well! They went to the field. And wonder of wonders, it was as Nanak had said. The neighbour's field showed no signs of being trampled. The crops rose thick and high. The owner was puzzled.

'How can it be?' he kept muttering to himself, Nanak told me later. 'I saw it with my own eyes!'

'And so did we!' Rai Bular said, laughing heartily. 'Your complaint is now null and void!'

Leaving him muttering away, my father and brother came home. I rejoiced secretly when I heard what had happened. The first signs had started! So what if the whole episode put Papaji in a bad mood for the rest of the week!

Rai Bular was not as rigid a man as my father. He realized there was something unusual going on. One of his attendants was a great friend of our servant Bala. One day, a few weeks later, I overheard the following conversation.

'Do you know what happened the other day?' Rai Bular's attendant said to Bala. 'Rai Bular himself saw a miracle!'

'Oh?' Bala said, dropping his work to listen.

'We were crossing the field to get to the *pradhan*'s house, when we saw Nanak lying as if dead on the grass. It was blazing noon, mind you, we could barely lift our eyes. Above the boy's body there stood an enormous cobra! "Snake! Snake!" they screamed, some of the timid ones among us and ran off. I didn't. In fact I was the one who realized that the boy was merely sleeping. So did Rai Bular.

'"Stop running, you fools!" he said. "Look carefully! The cobra hasn't bitten the boy. It's protecting him!"

'The fools stopped running. Rai Bular was right. In that blazing hot field, there was not an inch of shade. Except where Nanak lay. The great cobra was using his hood to give Nanak shade as he slept!

'With all this running and shouting, the cobra slipped off and disappeared somewhere. Feeling the sun on his head, Nanak woke up, and was surprised to see such a crowd around him. But no one was more surprised than us! For guess what Rai Bular did next?'

'What?' Bala said.

'He got off his horse and bent down and touched Nanak's feet! Can you imagine!'

I could. My brother was blessed. Three of us in the village knew it. Soon, more would.

I should have been happy, the way things were going. But Nanak worried me. He had become washed-out and thin. I searched his face for traces of that bouncy little boy I had raced about with. I found none. He avoided everyone, even me. Sometimes I caught him talking to himself. He would go out to do something and come back hours later, having completely forgotten what he had gone for or where he had been. The villagers started talking. Was Mehta Kalu's son going mad? These whispers reached my father.

One day, when Nanak was sitting at home for once, his plate of food untouched, Papaji sent for the village doctor. The doctor came and started checking Nanak's pulse. I hovered around, anxious. Was my dear Nanak ill?

Suddenly, Nanak came out of his reverie with a start and snatched back his hand. 'What are you doing?' he asked sharply.

'Finding out what is wrong with you, child,' the doctor answered. 'You are not well.'

To my horror, Nanak started to laugh. I think Papaji would have slapped him if he hadn't stopped laughing, as abruptly as he had started.

'How can you tell by feeling my pulse?' he said. 'Pain lies hidden deep in one's heart. Go and heal yourself before you try to cure others!'

The doctor was not at all offended by this outburst. Mad patients of his did this sort of thing all the time.

'So you think I am ill too, do you?' he said, good-humouredly.

'Who isn't?' my brother replied. 'Your soul is sick. You are too proud. Your ego keeps you from reaching the source of life, which is God.'

'What medicine should I take then?' the doctor said.

'Lose yourself in the name of the Bright One. Your body will become like gold and your soul will become pure. All pain and sorrow will vanish and you will be saved!'

These were clearly not the words of a mad man. Before long, the doctor was deep in discussion with the boy who was supposed to be his patient! Before he left, he said to my father, 'Your son needs no doctor. No, he himself will be the healer of countless souls!'

My father didn't know whether to be glad or angry. What use was all this business of saving souls when his son had not learnt a trade or anything that would help him stand on his own two feet! It was all too unrealistic. He had to put the boy back on track.

And so he called my brother the next day and said, 'Here, take these twenty rupees and go to the nearest town. Buy a few things that householders need and bring them back and sell them here at a profit. That is called doing business. Bala will go with you this time as it is your first.'

Poor Nanak! He had to obey Papaji. I packed some food for them and secretly told Bala to look after Nanak. They went off.

Around evening, Bala came back alone. My heart sank.

'Where's Nanak?' I said. 'Has something happened?'

'Nothing, Bibi Nanki,' Bala replied. 'He is afraid to come home.
He is sitting under the big tree outside the village.'

'What!' Papaji had arrived on the scene. 'What on earth for?'

And then the whole story came tumbling out. Halfway to the
next village, Nanak and Bala had run into a group of fakirs. The
fakirs had been travelling for days and were tired and hungry.

'Nanak Baba took one look at them and said to me, "Bala, I am
so glad we came. Take this money and hurry to the town. Buy all
the food you can and hurry back. Quick!" What could I do? It was
the young master's order. When I came back with the food, Nanak
Baba was talking to the fakirs as if they were his best friends! We
spent the whole day there. We talked and ate and the day passed
just like *that*!'

'I don't know which one's the bigger fool, you or my son!' Papaji
shouted. 'Wasting good money like that! Tell him to come home
at once! Hiding like a boy of two! He should be ashamed of himself!'

Bala went and brought Nanak home.

'Punish me however you like,' he said when Papaji scolded him.
'But it was a better bargain than the one you told me to make. Far,
far better!'

My father was at his wit's end. Schooling had failed. An attempt
at learning business had failed. Now the only hope was marriage. I
had already been married off the year before. It broke my heart to
leave Nanak, knowing how much he would irritate and annoy my

father without meaning to. I needn't have worried so much. Nanak, it seemed, was quite happy to get married, and so his wedding happened with much fanfare. I went back to my husband's house in Sultanpur with an easy mind. Maybe a wife and children were what my brother needed right now. Soon I had two beautiful nephews to play with when I came home to Talwandi. Had my brother become a householder after all?

But things had changed only on the surface. Nanak was as dreamy and impractical as ever. My father, older now, and more impatient than ever, couldn't cope with the disappointment. That's when I had a brilliant idea.

'Let me take him to Sultanpur, Papaji,' I said. 'My husband will get him a nice job, and once he settles down, Bhabhi and the two boys can join him.'

Papaji was visibly relieved. My husband was the dewan to Nawab Daulat Khan Lodhi, the Governor of Sultanpur. I would ask him to get my poor brother a job.

It all happened faster than I dared hope. Soon, Nanak had the job of storekeeper at the nawab's granary. To my father's eternal surprise, Nanak proved to be good at his job. He was efficient and honest and everyone liked him. My plan seemed to have worked. Till one day, it all went wrong.

Nanak went into a trance while counting and weighing provisions for the customers and started giving out grain, completely free! It was a disaster. The nawab was very angry when he heard the news. 'Sack the man, and count and see how much is missing!' he ordered. His officials arrived at the store and began taking stock. Nanak stood by and watched. To their great surprise, the officials could not find anything missing. Countless townspeople had gone off with sackfuls of grain, and still the stores were intact and the accounts in order! It was a miracle.

It was also the sign that Nanak had been waiting for. A householder's life was not for him, however much he tried. He went back to Talwandi. Papaji was too tired to even be angry any more. I alone felt content. Now at last my brother could follow his true calling.

One day, I received a frantic letter from home.

Nanak is missing, come quickly!

I rushed to Talwandi. Everyone was distraught. It seemed Nanak had gone off to bathe a few mornings ago in the river Baeen and not come back. Search parties combed the riverbank. I sat at home and prayed, wanting to run madly along the river, looking for him myself.

Two days passed, then three. I cooked, but no one ate. On the fourth day, the dawn was as grey as our faces. Suddenly Bala gave a great shout.

'It's him! He's back!'

My legs turned to water. I don't remember if I was crying or laughing. There he was, my dearest Nanak, his face radiant, smiling, a light circling his head like a halo. We asked him so many questions, we cried, we laughed, we gave him food, but Nanak just stayed that way, entranced, not talking, but brilliantly happy.

On the fifth day, he explained where he had been.

As he walked into the river, it seemed the water grew hands and pulled him down. The next thing he knew, he was standing in a fabulous place. It was the court of the Almighty who handed him a goblet brimming with nectar. 'Drink,' the Almighty commanded. He drank. Then the Almighty said, 'You have drunk of my Holy Name. Now go and do the work for which you were born. Spread my word, glorify my name. Spread the message of love and truth and destroy hypocrisy and sin.'

After telling us this much, Nanak fell silent again. I could see his hands were trembling. He was having trouble finding words to express what he had seen. He drank some water and spoke again, this time directly to me.

'If I lived a million years on air alone, if I lived in a dark cave and never saw the sun or the moon, if I were cut down like a tree or burned to ashes like firewood, if I became a bird that could fly to a hundred heavens or an invisible spirit that lived forever, if I had reams and reams of paper to write on and my ink never dried up and my pen moved like the wind, even then, Nanki, I could not express that Name in all its glory.'

But the Almighty had read his thoughts and His voice had said, 'It is simple. My name is God and you are my Guru. Be good to those I have blessed.'

'And then I found myself on the riverbank again, and I came home. And now I must go. I have work to do.'

My father wept to see him go. So did I. For once, our tears were shed for the same reason. We were both proud of Nanak and happy that he should have been chosen to wear the robe of the Lord's praise and prayer, and drink from the goblet of His name. Nanak's family was now made up of all tribes and races. My little brother Nanak was now Guru Nanak, minstrel of God.

Wherever he went, he preached oneness. It was he who taught us that there is no difference between man and man, that we are all one in prayer, in deed and in truth. The light that once I alone had seen would now shine throughout the world.

THE TRIAL
OF FAITH

The **ghostly hand** wrote a few words **on the wall.**

*W*ith a great grinding, the stone was pushed into place. Many feet of solid rock behind me. Before me, the lions.

I had seen this coming. For a long time, they had disliked us, the favourites from Jerusalem, Nebuchadnezzar's golden boys. How they envied us for just being who we were! We hadn't asked to be taken away from our mothers, taken away from our city, and brought here, to Babylon! And yet, they hated us.

Not Nebuchadnezzar. He loved us from the day we were brought into court. He had to. He thought of us as his sons. The children of Chaldea! I remember those first bewildered days, the food so different, suddenly the robes of silk that felt hot and tight, not like the loose cotton robes we romped about in at home. And the strangeness! The strange faces, the strange tongues, words that seemed to be shaped of air for all the sense they made to our ears! I remember even the soldiers who came to take us.

'Your sons will be loved like the king's own. After all, he is now King of Judea, and like a father to you all! Your son, we have heard, is bright. He will do well at the court. And you, their mothers, will be proud!'

My mother had crushed me in her arms, so reluctant was she to let me go, and yet so convinced that the king's soldiers could mean no harm. And in truth, they didn't. They took us to the Babylonian king's palace and gave us new clothes and fed us new food out of plates we had never seen the likes of! I liked the plates better than the food they served on them.

'Meat from the king's kitchen,' the prince in charge of us boys told us. 'Eat and grow healthy!' But I could not eat that food. The others thought I was stupid to refuse such delicious meat. All except Hananiah, Mishael and Azariah. In their faces I saw my own distaste.

With my three new friends, I had stepped up to the grand prince, and said, 'Please sir prince, we do not wish to eat the meat that is served us!'

Horror! Heavens! The other boys thought we would be chained, or whipped, or worse.

But the prince was not so unkind. He said, 'What will I tell the king if he sees you looking feeble? He will behead me if he knows I have disobeyed him. What then?'

And I answered, 'Give us ten days. For ten days serve us pulses instead of meat and water instead of wine. At the end of ten days, if we look feeble, then punish us!'

The prince agreed. When our ten days were over, he lined us all up and looked at us carefully. He pinched our cheeks and turned us from side to side. I felt like a horse! And then he said, 'It is strange! You look fatter, and fairer than the rest! You win. You four boys shall eat whatever you please!'

It was my first victory in Babylon and it felt sweet! They taught us well. I learnt hungrily, for I had always yearned to know more. I learnt science and language, art and music. We four friends stuck together. It was as good a life as could be expected in a strange land.

And then he called us to court. 'King Nebuchadnezzar will see you tomorrow,' our prince told us, a nervous wobble in his voice. 'I am proud of you, and I hope he will be too!'

Court was much as I had imagined. Opulent and showy, full of princes who preened and followers who fawned. The king was oblivious to their attentions. He watched us keenly as we entered and bowed. And then, one by one, he questioned us on all we had learnt. Soon we noticed he was questioning only us four. Not questioning so much as conversing. The king was conversing with us boys! What did we care, we stood as we always did, straight and tall, and answered as we always have, swift and unafraid. No fawning for us! It impressed the king. Much to the dismay of his court astrologers and magicians, he announced, 'From this day, Daniel, Shadrach, Meshach and Abednego (for these were the names he called Hananiah, Mishael and Azariah by) will be my favourite counsellors!'

That's when the hatred started.

The lions have only just realized what has entered their den. Meat. Human meat. The bars no longer confine them. I hear the first growl, see the first flick of the tail. I stay where I am.

Two years passed. One day, puzzling news reached me. King

Nebuchadnezzar has ordered the court magicians and astrologers to be put to death! Why? I hurried to Arioch, the captain of the guards and asked him what had happened. 'They have failed to tell the king what he has dreamt,' Arioch told me. 'You are wise, Daniel. How can anyone tell what has appeared in another person's dream? It is impossible! And so because they have failed this impossible task, he wants them dead!'

'Let me talk to him,' I said, and hurried to the court.

'I had a disquieting dream last night,' the king told me. 'But try as I might, I cannot recall it. And these nincompoop men of mine say they cannot tell me, it is impossible.'

'Give me one night,' I said to him, 'and I will tell you both your dream and its meaning.'

It was big-headed of me to do it, but I couldn't let those men die, however much they disliked me. I went home and prayed all night and in the morning I was ready.

They were waiting, waiting for me to fail. I looked only at the king.

'The secret that your wise men and soothsayers could not reveal has been revealed to me, O King, by my God. This is what you saw. A great statue, ominously tall. Its head was of fine gold, its chest and arms of silver, its belly and thighs of brass, its legs of iron, and its feet of iron and clay. As you looked at this giant image, a massive stone came out of nowhere and broke it to pieces. And then, the stone that broke the statue became a great mountain and filled the earth. Am I not right, O king?'

King Nebuchadnezzar nodded. The magicians and soothsayers looked stunned. I continued.

'Well then, this is what it means. It is a message from God, who has given you a kingdom, and with it power and glory. You are the head of gold, O King, for right now you are the brightest and most powerful king of all. But after you, another king will come, inferior to you, as silver is inferior to gold and then another, whose kingdom shall be like brass. The fourth kingdom will be like iron, strong and harsh. And the toes of iron and clay shall be the next kingdom, which will be partly strong and partly weak. As all these kings rule, another kingdom will be created in heaven which will never be destroyed. But the earthly ones will be broken into pieces by the same God that made them powerful once.'

King Nebuchadnezzar listened, stupefaction growing in his eyes, and with it, respect. At last, he rose and bowed before me, so that the entire court gasped with the shock and unseemliness of it and he announced, 'Daniel shall be the chief of all the wise men in the country. He will sit by my right hand, and shall be second only to the king! Is that understood by all?'

And the court raised a big 'Yea!' but I knew their hearts were burning.

The king misunderstood my explanation. Pleased at the thought of being the 'golden king' of the dream, he ordered a giant statue of gold to be made in his likeness. It was a giant folly—ninety feet tall and nine feet wide.

The day it was ready, he called all his governors, judges, treasurers, counsellors and rulers from all his provinces and gathered them before the statue. A herald blew a trumpet and announced that every day, when the flutes and harps and zithers were played, all the people in the kingdom were to fall on their knees before the golden image and worship it. Anyone who failed to do so would be thrown into a furnace. And then the harps and flutes and zithers were played, and everyone fell down and worshipped the image.

Naturally, the four of us did not. The courtiers were afraid of me, but Shadrach, Meshach and Abednego had not been singled out and favoured as openly as I had been. So they turned their spite against them.

'The three Jews you have made governors of Babylon, they have not worshipped your golden image.'

'They have disobeyed your orders!'

'They must be punished!'

Perhaps King Nebuchadnezzar felt angrier because Shadrach, Meshach and Abednego were his favourites. He loved them, and they openly flouted his commands. Determined not to be soft, the king ordered the furnace to be heated at seven times its normal temperature. 'I will roast the rebels alive!' he declared. I said nothing. It was a trial. I just wished it was happening to me, instead of my dearest boyhood friends, my own Hananiah, Mishael and Azariah!

Well, I got my chance. This trial is mine alone. The first lion gets up. Not thinking, I take a step towards him.

The flames burst upwards from the furnace. The crowd yelped. The men who had tied up Shadrach, Meshach and Abednego had been swallowed by the fire. Dead. We all looked closely at the furnace, King Nebuchadnezzar the closest.

And there, where by now my three friends' charred corpses should have been, were four men walking in the red-hot furnace!

The king's bafflement was written all over his face. Three of them were Shadrach, Meshach and Abednego, but how had they freed themselves? And who was the fourth? He looked heavenly. Where had he sprung from? I alone knew and I gave thanks, silently, in my heart.

The king couldn't take it any more. Trembling, he went up to the furnace and called them out. Out they stepped, my dearest friends. Not a hair was singed, not one had a single burn on his body! And right there, King Nebuchadnezzar praised the god who sent his angel to protect his believers, and announced a new decree. From that day on, all the people in his kingdom were to worship no other god but that of Shadrach, Meshach and Abednego.

Life would have been good, if the king had not had another disquieting dream.

'I saw a mighty tree that reached up to heaven,' he said to me. 'And then I saw it being cut down and left as an ugly stump with an iron band around it. I was so afraid!'

My answer did nothing to reassure him.

'The tree you saw O King,' I said, 'which was mighty and strong, whose leaves were green and fruit ripe, which gave shadow to the beasts of the field and shelter to the birds of heaven—that tree is you. For your strength has grown much, and your kingdom is large. But the highest ruler of all knows that you have been cruel and unjust to the weak and defenceless. Repent, the God of heaven says, or else your rule shall be cut down like that tree and you will be at the mercy of the elements!'

He heard me out, but he didn't say a word. I could tell he was displeased. One year later, when he walked into the palace of Babylon, he was overcome by pride.

'Is this not Great Babylon that I myself have built, and that honours me and worships my majesty?' he exclaimed.

But even as he spoke, a voice came out of heaven saying, 'Nebuchadnezzar! Your rule has ended!'

And so indeed it had. The prophecy had come true and he himself had caused it. The king, once so powerful, was driven away into the fields where he ate grass like the cattle and slept, shivering, under a blanket of dew. His hair grew long like an eagle's feathers and his nails grew as sharp as a bird's claws.

At the end of this long hard time, at last Nebuchadnezzar lifted his eyes to heaven and praised the lord, for he had realized that nothing was his without God's blessing. And as he prayed, his kingdom was restored and his counsellors came flocking back and installed him on the throne once more.

I retired to a life of peace and prayer. What else can an old man do?

After Nebuchadnezzar's death, his son Belshazzar ascended the throne and gave a great feast. I did not go to the feast but I was told how lavish it was. Lavish, and foolish. For the occasion, the young king commanded that the vessels his father had taken from the temple of Jerusalem be brought to the banquet hall. It was done, and Belshazzar and his wives, princes and courtiers drank wine from the gold and silver vessels, and praised the gods of gold and silver.

Suddenly in the midst of all this revelry, the fingers of a disembodied hand appeared against the wall of the banquet hall. Everyone screamed. As they watched, the ghostly hand wrote a few words on the wall. The king, I was told, turned ashen. His hands shook. His goblet fell to the floor.

'Send for the astrologers and the soothsayers!' he cried. 'Whoever can tell me what this writing means will be clothed in scarlet robes and given a chain of gold for his neck!'

It was Belshazzar's queen who remembered me. A gentle and thoughtful woman, she said to him, 'There is a man who in your father's time was known for his wisdom and understanding. King Nebuchadnezzar made him the master of all his wise men. Let him be called and he will tell you what this means.'

And so they sent for me. 'Keep your gifts to yourself, O King,' I said to him. 'I will willingly read the writing on the wall. It is a warning from the God whose breath gives you life. Your father was a great king. But even he was lesser than the King in heaven. You, his son, O Belshazzar, are proud and unthinking. You have not acknowledged your Master. Instead you have tried to take His place. You have drunk wine out of His sacred vessels and praised the gods of gold. Your reign is finished. Your kingdom is to be divided between the Medeans and the Persians. You have lost your last chance to save yourself.'

Saying this, I left the court.

That very same night, Belshazzar, King of the Chaldeans, was killed and Darius the Medean ruler took over his kingdom.

It seems I was to have no peace. The new king installed one hundred and twenty princes to rule over different parts of his kingdom. Above these princes he placed three presidents and he made me the first among the three.

'I had heard of you in my homeland, Daniel,' he said to me. 'There's no one I trust more than you.'

I now had one hundred and twenty princes and two presidents against me.

I have nothing against you, I think. Stay. A dreadful growling starts. My thoughts are no good in this den. The lions cannot read my thoughts.

How zealously they watched me, my one hundred and twenty-two enemies! If only they had been as zealous in their work! They watched my every move. One slip-up, one fault, and I would be dead. But they waited and waited in vain, and grew angrier and angrier.

I waited too. I knew they would force things to a head. And just as I had thought, one day, as I knelt before my open window, facing Jerusalem, city of my heart, and prayed, three times as I have done for all these years of my life, the summons came.

'You are under arrest!' the guards shouted roughly. 'We are to take you to the king at once.'

I went. King Darius looked distressed beyond words.

'Daniel! Forgive me for what I am about to do to you. I was a fool to listen to the men I thought were worthy. Forgive me!'

And then he told me. The plotters had made him sign a petition saying that whoever prays to any god or man other than King Darius was to be thrown into a lions' den. Then they had rushed guards to my house, at the time they knew I prayed, and brought me to be punished.

'The law of the Persians, once made, cannot be broken, Daniel,' the king said, sorrowfully. 'If only I had guessed their evil intent. Forgive me!'

And then the guards pinned my arms to my side and threw me into the deepest dungeons where the starving lions roared, starved by the plotters for my sake, trapped and ravenous for me.

With a great grinding, the stone was pushed into place. Many feet of solid rock behind me. Before me, the lions.

I have nowhere else to look but into their eyes. I look, and the first lion stares back. It is an intense confrontation, man and lion, frail human and magnificent beast. Suddenly I am not afraid. I am ready for what must come.

Morning brought with it the sound of a voice. A human voice. King Darius, calling from the other side of the stone. Broken, raw emotion seeping through the stone. 'Daniel! What have I done to you! May you and your God forgive me!'

The man was suffering.

I cried out, 'Grieve not, O King! Remove the rock and see me with your own eyes!'

Silence. Was I hearing voices? Had I crossed over to the afterworld?

And then the grinding sound of the stone. And the metal whine of the bars that had sealed the lions in, and been raised to let them loose on me. Whining, they slid back into place. I could have told them, let it be. The bars aren't needed any more. We sat the whole night, the lions and I, and they did not hurt me. Not a scratch. We sat, and it was as if we had spoken.

The king embraced me when I emerged. He had a look in his eye. The same look King Nebuchadnezzar had that first time I told him his dream. That very day he sent out a proclamation throughout his vast kingdom: 'All men of all languages and all nations should worship the God of Daniel. The God who delivered Daniel from the mouth of the lions, the God who hushed those hungry beasts and bathed Daniel in a ray of godly light.'

And so my faith became theirs and I lived on, treasured companion, counsellor and friend throughout the reign of King Darius the Medean and the reign of King Cyrus the Persian after him.

They had saved the

darkest
dungeon
for me.

There they sit, shooting questions at me like arrows. I don't mind. In fact, I welcome it. What a wonderful chance to prove myself. I, the boy who once had so many questions of my own, and no one to answer them! Let the questions come.

. . .

Who made the sun and the moon? What makes the wind blow and the water flow? Why is summer hot and the winter bitterly cold? Who made me, these untamed valleys and my father's sheep?

As a young boy, these questions would worry me as much as the beauty of my surroundings enthralled me. I had four brothers, two older and two younger, but I felt as if I were all alone. No one else seemed interested in questions like those. They were happy running wild across the hills all day and slurping huge bowls of soup before falling fast asleep each night. My father had no time for my questions, and my mother, kind soul though she was, had no answers.

My questions grew a bit more difficult as I grew up. Nature was hard to understand but at least it was beautiful. The people I saw around me were not. What made them fight and kill each other? What made them lie to their best friends and steal from their neighbours? Why did some people have so much wealth and some so little? The more I saw of the world I lived in, the less I understood it.

Lonely and questioning, I grew up to be a man of thirty. One night, I was tossing and turning in bed, unable to sleep. The night was quiet. Far away, a watchful dog barked. Finding it impossible to lie down any longer, I was about to get up and sit outside, when a dazzling being appeared, towering before me in the dark. If I hadn't been so wide awake, I would have thought I was dreaming.

'Who are you?' I asked.

'I am Vohu Manah, the Angel of Good Thought,' the dazzling being said. 'Come with me, Zarathushtra, and I will show you the answers to all your questions.'

I took the dazzling being's hand and in an instant, I was no longer in my own room. I was transported to a space that seemed to have no beginning or end. For a man who had never stopped marvelling at how beautiful the clear blue skies of his childhood were, here was beauty beyond words. Seven angels, their faces glowing with kindness, greeted me.

'We are the Amesha Spentas,' they said, their voices sweet and clear as bells. 'We are the creations of Ahura Mazda, the one God who has made everything that is good on earth. The skies, the seas, the trees, all that you, Zarathushtra, have loved so dearly, are His creations. He makes the winds blow and the waters flow. He puts heat in the rays of the sun and cold in the snows of winter.'

I listened. My heart hammered in my throat.

'But you are thinking—if Ahura Mazda made what's good, who made what's evil?'

I nodded. Words had failed me completely.

'It is Angra Mainyu who brought all the things that pain your heart, Zarathushtra,' the Amesha Spentas said. 'Anger and hatred, cruelty and crime. He causes them all. He is chaos. He is the opposite of Ahura Mazda. Where the Wise Lord seeks harmony, Angra Mainyu seeks destruction. But in the end, even he will be defeated by good. Now come with us and we will show you the past, the present and the future.'

The Amesha Spentas took me by the hand and revealed to me how Ahura Mazda breathed life into the world by casting light into an abyss. They showed me how the Wise Lord created them, the Amesha Spentas, out of His own spirit and made them responsible for each of the seven creations. The sky, the sea, the earth, the plants, animals, man and finally, a brilliant ray of fire, which was the everlasting light of Ahura. They showed me the birth of the first man and the first woman, and how they believed the first lie. And at last they showed me the bridge we would all have to cross at the end of our lives, and how the bridge would become narrower and narrower for the wicked, and broader and brighter for the good people as they walked upright into heaven.

And then they turned solemnly to me and they spoke.

'Why have we brought you here, why have we shown you all these wonders? These are the questions in your mind, are they not, Zarathushtra? The answer is this—you are Ahura Mazda's chosen messenger. You will spread the word of the one true God and guide people away from their evil ways and their false gods. You have been instructed well. Now go and be worthy of your task.'

'But I fear I may not be worthy,' I said, finding my tongue at last. 'How will I teach what is so vast and so difficult?'

'We shall make it simple for you, O mortal,' said the Amesha Spentas. 'Good thoughts, good words, good deeds. Let these three be your guide wherever you go and whatever you preach.'

And before I knew it, I was back in my cold bed. No one stirred, and far away, the watchful dog still barked.

. . .

'Test him, O King,' the priests of King Hyspastes had said, after he had heard me out. 'Allow us to question him, so we can tell if he is truly a prophet as he claims, or a fraud, as we believe.'

The king, who seemed like a good man, had nodded. He depended heavily on his priests, I could tell. And besides, he had a right to doubt me. What I said was not agreeable, because I spoke the truth. Everyone doubted me. Why else was I here, so far away from home, surrounded by cold and suspicious eyes?

. . .

All night I thought of what I had heard and seen. When morning came, I could hardly wait to tell my family and fellow villagers.

'Stop these senseless sacrifices,' I told the priests, who were the most powerful people in our village. 'Ahura Mazda asks for good deeds, not slaughtered lambs.'

But the priests were enraged, for no one had dared question their rituals before. That didn't stop me.

'Throw away your drinking bowls and pitchers of wine,' I told the noblemen. 'Wine makes you sluggish and stupid. Keep your mind clear and you will find yourself uttering good words, and Ahura Mazda will bless you!'

But the noblemen paid no attention, for who was I to stop them from having a good time?

'Don't raise your hand in haste and your voice in anger,' I told the villagers. 'It displeases Ahura Mazda, who is our true God, and it brings you no peace. Instead of filling your heart with hatred, fill your mind with good thoughts. And then see how joyful life will be!'

But the villagers merely mocked me, because what use were good thoughts against bad neighbours?

The more earnestly I tried to spread the message of Ahura Mazda, the more opposition I faced. The priests declared me an impostor and an outcast. The nobles threatened to snatch away my land. But the villagers were the worst, for they made every moment of every day sheer misery for me. The village had been my home all my life, but now it was suddenly alien to me. No one wanted me there, I could tell by the contempt in their eyes and the derision in their voices. If they were to have their own way, I would be dead and my teachings snuffed out for good.

That's when I had the dream. The angel Vohu Manah came to me in the night and said, 'Flee from here, Zarathushtra! Take your horses and camels and the twenty-two faithfuls who have accepted your word, and fly east. Go before dawn breaks and the priests' henchmen descend on you with sticks.'

I remember the icy clutch of sadness at my heart. My life was being uprooted. Unsure about where to go, but knowing I must, I left the village before dawn with a small band of men and animals.

We followed the path wherever it led us. The land was savage, few plants grew, and our small flock soon died of hunger and thirst. I felt abandoned. 'Where shall I go, Lord?' I cried out at night, while the rest tried to huddle into sleep. 'To whom shall I turn? Show me, for I am lost and weary!'

He heard my prayers. After all those weeks of trudging eastward, we found ourselves here, in the kingdom of a kind king. From now on, things could only get better.

. . .

I debated with the priests for days. It raged on, and nothing I said seemed to satisfy them. Thirty-three questions they asked me, and thirty-three times I answered, as simply and patiently as I could. I had nothing to lose. The more they doubted, the more I was certain, and some of this must have shown on my face. For finally, when the priests declared the debate to be over, the king turned to me with a generous smile.

'This young man speaks of good things,' he said. 'Let us give his new faith a chance!'

But the priests would not hear of it.

'He is not as sincere as he appears, Your Highness,' they told him. 'It is not a new faith that he comes to teach. No! It is your throne he is interested in, O King. He hopes to win you with his pleasant words and have us, your loyal supporters, thrown out of the court. Then he will overthrow Your Highness and occupy the throne himself. Do not let his youth or his sweet speech deceive you. Do not let him poison you against us, who have proven our allegiance. Follow our advice and have him thrown into prison.'

Prison! The word clanged around my ears. I looked at the king. He was struggling with his own kind intentions. Maybe he was too trusting. Maybe this Zarathushtra was not as blameless as he seemed. Why else had he been driven away from his homeland? The priests had never misled him before. Why should they do so now? And so, relying on the priests' crooked advice, King Hyspastes had me thrown into chains.

They had saved the darkest dungeon for me. Not a single chink of light entered the cell, and not a breath of air stirred. The floor was damp and cold, and crawled with things that I could not see, but could sense in the pitch dark. My legs and arms were chained, and when I moved, my skin rubbed against the chains and bled. Every day, my jailors devised new ways of increasing my pain. One day they would deprive me of water altogether. The next day they would pour buckets of water through the bars till it came up to my neck, and I almost drowned. They dangled food before my lips and then snatched it out of reach. They unchained me only to prod me, blinking, into the sun, where they whipped me and left me standing motionless in the sweltering heat. They fed me charred insects and dead rats. They spat on my face and twisted my hair. Their greatest delight seemed to lie in inventing newer, crueller ways to torment me, so they could have the pleasure of watching me beg to be released.

I did not grant them that pleasure.

One of the guards, who later became my friend, told me how irate my calm acceptance of all their tortures made them. 'The more tranquil you looked,' he said, 'the more we would want to humiliate you. Beat and bruise you till you cried out or lashed back. But nothing! Just a light that seemed to come from your face. The more you suffered, the more the light seemed to shine. It was as if your body was a window to your soul. That window had been flung open and light streamed out, as if from the sun! How it drove us mad!'

I did not know any of this. All I knew was the endless reservoir of strength inside me that kept me going, no matter what.

One day, the guards were less attentive than usual. I soon found out why. The king's favourite warhorse had apparently fallen ill without any reason. One day it was in perfect health, the next day it was ill. 'Such a splendid beast, all gleaming skin and rippling muscles, in such a bad shape!' the guards said to each other, ignoring me for once. 'Its ribs stick out, its hair has fallen off in clumps, and worst of all, its legs are paralysed. The king has sent for his best healers. They have tried everything—every potion, every poultice, every brew. Nothing has worked. So abject has the king become that he has begun sacrificing a thousand camels and horses every day, beseeching the gods to save his precious horse.'

'And still nothing works!'

I raised my voice and asked to see the king.

'At last, you miserable wretch,' they said. 'At last you admit you are a fraud!'

'Nothing of the sort,' I said. 'It's just that I can help cure the king's horse!'

'That's a clever way to get out of here,' one of the guards sniggered. 'Catch our king falling for that one!'

But I knew King Hyspastes would see me. His better instincts had always opposed my imprisonment. Besides, he was so worried, he would seize any chance of hope.

Just as I thought, he arrived at my cell to hear what I had to say.

'Grant my wishes, O King,' I said, 'and your horse will be cured.'

'Name your wishes,' the king said.

'Simply that you, Your Highness, your queen, your ministers and all your courtiers give up your false gods and follow Ahura Mazda.'

'Done!' said the king and ordered me to be released at once and accompanied to new rooms in the palace. Then he rushed back to the stables to see if he had been tricked. The soft sound of whinnying greeted him. Standing on all fours in the middle of the stable was his horse, his coat gleaming, his hooves impatient, his head thrown back as proudly as only a king's warhorse could be!

No further proof was needed. No further plots and priestly schemes could change the king's mind. He accepted my faith, and so did all his noblemen.

My joy was inexpressible. I had at last been worthy of Ahura Mazda's trust in me.

One day, soon after, He sent a sign. We were all gathered in the court when suddenly a pillar of flame blazed out of the floor. The courtiers leapt back, afraid of getting burnt. Even the king looked startled. But then Ahura Mazda's voice emerged from the flames and said, 'Fear not, O illustrious king! This is my sign that Zarathushtra is indeed my chosen prophet, and his faith the true and right religion. It is my wish that you follow his words and fill the earth with my glory!' The fire vanished and everyone fell on their faces in awe.

From then on, I lived in the court of King Hyspastes. I had found my true home at last. Of one thing I made sure. Anyone, any time, could come to me with a question. No matter how big or small the question, or how tired or busy I was, I would try and answer it. It was my homage to the God that chose me, an untaught shepherd boy, to be a prophet. It was my way of giving Him thanks.

THE FLIGHT
OF THE
PERSECUTED

Fools! They race towards their own death!

made Moses. He was born a slave but I made him a noble. He could have inherited all the riches of Egypt, but all he inherited was the wilderness. He saved his people, but they cursed him. Why did he do it? I never understood, not even now, as my whole life passes before my eyes and I know I have only moments to live.

My Israelite slaves were useful, but exasperating. The rate at which they multiplied, one day we Egyptians would find ourselves outnumbered! And yet I couldn't get rid of them, I needed them. The pyramids were yet to be built, and I had so many other plans! But they didn't make me Pharaoh for nothing! I knew a better way of curbing their outrageous growth. I called the midwives and said, 'If an Israelite gives birth to a boy, put it to death immediately. Only newborn girls must be allowed to live!' The midwives nodded and went away. And yet I got news that the number of male children in the Hebrew camp of Geshon was on the rise.

I summoned the midwives again.

'How dare you disobey me?' I thundered. 'Why are you letting the boys live?'

'It is not our fault!' they whimpered in return. 'It is the Hebrew women. They are so strong and healthy that they don't need us. By the time we arrive, their boys are already born and hidden away from us. What can we do to prevent it, O Pharaoh!'

I knew they were lying. But I couldn't punish them without proof. So I made a public proclamation.

'Listen, all my people!' I announced. 'All of you, be you Egyptian or Hebrew, slave or prince, must cast your sons into the Nile. Daughters you may raise, but sons you may not!'

I know, the plan had flaws. It meant that Egyptian families would not grow either. But sometimes, such sacrifices are called for. That is what being a Pharaoh means.

My spies brought me good news. My guards roamed all the quarters. Male babies were not to be seen any more, they informed me.

'Good,' I said.

And then suddenly my daughter came home with a child, a boy-child, and begged me to let her keep it. I was extremely aggravated.

'Where did you get this boy?' I shouted.

'Father, listen, he is a gift from the Nile itself!' my daughter said, a tremulous agitation in her voice. 'I had gone to bathe this morning as usual, when I saw this basket of bulrushes hidden among the reeds. My maids brought it to me, and when I opened it and saw the sweetest child wrapped up in a blanket and crying his heart out, I couldn't let him go! Please, Father, let me keep him! The gods want us to!'

That's when I made my biggest mistake. I relented. Of course I had a sound reason for doing so, or else I wouldn't be Pharaoh, but now I realize I would have done better to have that child thrown back into the Nile. He was no gift from the gods! He was some clever Hebrew mother's child, who must have known about my daughter's tender nature and placed the basket where she would be sure to see it. But by then, it was too late. I relented and my daughter's smile of gratitude made it seem like I had done the right thing. Besides, (for that is how I reasoned at that time) I had no heir. This foundling could be made to become worthy of a Pharaoh. A Hebrew nurse was employed (a dying man's instinct tells me she must have been the boy's natural mother, so wily are the Hebrews), and my daughter raised him as her own son.

A very fine boy he turned out to be! I hired the best teachers for him. He learnt everything. Military manoeuvres, administration, literature, music, even architecture (we Pharaohs are great builders). He was an apt pupil. The Hebrew's natural intelligence, combined with the Egyptian's natural refinement, brought out the best in him. He was a warrior and a charmer. His words were as expressive as his sword. His bearing grew more and more regal, and his personality compelling. He was as fluent in the ancient wisdom of the Egyptians as he was in our languages. I couldn't have been prouder of him if he had been my own son.

And then he bit the hand that fed him. One day, he wandered into the campsite where the Hebrew slaves were at work. What he told me did not match what the guard on duty had to say. According to the guard, it was the slave's fault, *he* was just doing his job, keeping the lazy slobs moving. According to Moses, now officially declared my Crown Prince, future hope of the Pharaohs, it was the guard's fault.

'The bricks they made the slaves carry were too heavy, it was inhuman! A poor slave stumbled and the Egyptian began cursing him. When the poor slave raised his voice in protest, the guard began whipping him, mercilessly. I couldn't just stand and watch,' Moses told me indignantly. 'After all, they are my people. So I struck the cruel guard down!'

'That was foolish of you,' I told him. 'You are to be their Pharaoh, not their protector! Now they will think you are weak, and despise you!'

'Then I cannot be their Pharaoh,' he said, and he walked out of the court.

All my years of training betrayed by the ties of blood! Moses had turned his back on everything I had to offer him. He had offended the great line of Pharaohs, of whom he had been privileged to be a part. He wanted to be the Hebrews' saviour, but they would spurn him, as unthinkingly as he had spurned me.

I would have my revenge yet. One is not Pharaoh for nothing.

I had read the Hebrews right. The same guard that Moses had struck came back to me the next day, chortling.

'They have rejected Moses!' he said, triumphantly. 'He came

there today just when two of the slaves were fighting over some petty thing. He broke through the circle of men, like a big hero, and begged them not to hurt each other. "Why fight your own brother?" he said. "Fight those that oppress you!" But the Hebrew who had started the fight pushed Moses away and shouted, "Go away and leave us to do as we wish. Who made you a ruler and judge over us?" You should have seen his face! He was no hero after all! He turned away, looking like a sad fool and walked away. I would guess, O Pharaoh, that is the last we shall see of him!'

I waved the guard away. I wasn't so sure. Something told me that Moses and I had unfinished business.

I was right. I lose count of the years that passed in between. But I remember as if it were yesterday, the way I felt when I heard: 'Moses asks for an audience with the Pharaoh. He is back, and he has something important to say.'

'He returns to ask forgiveness,' I thought to myself. I must say the idea pleased me. It is pleasant when a Pharaoh gets a chance to be magnanimous.

'I will see him,' I said.

He walked in. My first reaction was shock. The Moses I knew was a dashing young man of forty, elegantly attired, sleek and stylish. The Moses who walked in was a patriarch. His hair had grown long, his beard unkempt. He looked like a man of the wilds. His robes were common, his staff rustic. Where had all my careful grooming gone?

'We have missed you,' I said, hoping to soften the discomfort he surely felt at being in such superior surroundings again. 'Let my servants attend to you first, and then we will talk.'

'I thank you, Pharaoh,' he said, his voice more commanding than I remembered. 'But my business is urgent. I have a request to make of you.'

'By all means,' I said, magnanimously. 'But first, tell me where you had hidden yourself all these years.'

'In the land of Midian, Pharaoh,' Moses answered. 'But that is of no importance. The real—'

'And what did you do there?' I interrupted.

'I tended my father-in-law's sheep,' Moses answered, beginning to look uneasy, for the conversation was not going his way.

'Oh! Then you are married! With sons?'

He nodded.

'And have you brought them with you, so we may see them?' I was enjoying teasing him, he looked so lost in that once-familiar court.

'No, Pharaoh, I come alone, with a message from my God. Allow my people into the desert for three days that we may honour our God with a feast.'

I was piqued. He had failed to observe the niceties of conversation. He had been crude enough to get to the point so hurriedly.

'And who is your god that he should command *me*, the Pharaoh?' I snapped. If he could be brusque, I could be cutting.

'A kind God and a wise one,' Moses answered, looking lost no longer. 'For He is giving you a chance to save your people from great harm. Release the Israelites or you will face His wrath!'

I could not take this tone from the boy who owed me everything, even his life. I dismissed him at once, and sent word to the camps. 'The slaves are to be worked harder! No rest, no meals, no mercy!'

Moses would soon find out he was not welcome.

'"Go back to the desert, old man!" they shouted,' my informer told me. '"You are back and we are being punished. Spare us and go!"'

But he didn't. The next day he was back at court, this time with a man he called his brother. Aaron was his name.

I decided to provoke him.

'What made you decide to play saviour?' I asked. 'Who chose you? Or are you self-appointed?'

'I was chosen by the burning bush,' he answered.

'Ah, a burning bush!' I repeated, sarcastically.

'It burned and yet it was not burnt!' Moses continued, as if he hadn't heard my barb. 'I was astonished. Not a branch snapped or crumbled into ash! I stepped closer when a voice said, "Stay! Do not come any closer. I am the God of your fathers! The God of Abraham, Isaac and Jacob! Do not be afraid!" But I hid my face in my hands, for I did not dare look at my Lord! He said to me in tongues of flame, "I have heard the cry of my people and I have come to deliver them from the Egyptians and take them to a land of milk and honey. And I have chosen you, Moses, to lead them. Go to the Pharaoh and ask him to set your people free!" And so, here I am, standing before you!'

It was as if he were possessed. His beard crackled as if with the mysterious fire he had just described, and his eyes sparked. I was impressed. He had been such good Pharaoh material! But now he was my enemy.

'How do I know you speak the truth?' I asked.

'Here is a sign,' he said, and his brother Aaron flung down his staff, which at once turned into a serpent.

I called my magicians. 'Can you do what Moses' brother Aaron has done?' I said.

In answer, all my magicians flung down their staffs at once, and they all turned into serpents. But then, before I could exult, Aaron's serpent swallowed up all the rest, and my magicians were powerless to stop it.

'Now will you let my people go?' Moses asked.

'No!' I thundered. 'Leave! And never return.'

211

'Then prepare yourself, Pharaoh,' Moses said. 'The Ten Plagues are coming! You will take back your words before long.'

'Never!' I roared, and that, I thought, was that.

Not so. The First Plague turned the beautiful blue waters of the Nile into blood. Fish died and floated downstream. No one bathed or washed. Then the women discovered that all the water stored in their houses had also turned into blood. Not a drop of water was to be had. For seven days, my people went thirsty, and still I did not agree.

And then Moses threatened me with the Second Plague. Millions of frogs appeared overnight, and filled our beds and our pools and our streams and our streets. Not an inch of space was free of the hopping croaking leaping things. I was more amused than alarmed. 'My magicians can outdo the second plague themselves,' I declared. 'Conjure up frogs and show Moses his god is but a magician!'

My magicians conjured up the frogs, but they could not make them disappear. At last, when I couldn't take the slimy creatures any more, I called Moses.

'Tell your god to take the frogs away, and I will let your people go.'

Fool! He agreed. The frogs vanished as suddenly as they had appeared, and I laughed in Moses' face. My slaves would never run free.

The Third Plague was a swarm of gnats. It was as if all the dust of

Egypt had suddenly been turned into a teeming swarm that buzzed and drove us mad. They got into our hair and eyes, and tormented men and beasts alike. My magicians panicked. 'This is the work of God, we cannot copy it. Let the Hebrews go,' they said.

But I would die before I agreed.

The Fourth Plague was worse. Great broods of dog-flies blotted out the sun next morning. They didn't just buzz, they bit. They sucked blood and laid eggs and multiplied and ate their way through everything. Garbage overflowed. The city stank.

If there's one thing Pharaohs hate, it's a stink. I called Moses and said, 'Take your men and make your sacrifice here in Egypt itself.'

But he said, 'The land is polluted, I must go into the desert where the air and earth are clean.'

I was so desperate I agreed. But when the swarms of bloodthirsty flies vanished, so did my desperation. I ignored Moses' plea.

It went on and on! The Fifth Plague killed our livestock. A terrible moaning and bleating filled the air as cows and goats, camels and sheep dropped dead wherever they were. Only the Hebrews were spared. Their livestock thrived. It was uncanny. I hardened my heart.

The Sixth Plague was heinous. A fine soot descended from the sky and clung to our skin which erupted into a frenzy of boils. Great big boils filled with pus that oozed and burst and erupted in new places. No one emerged from their homes. Moses threatened me with even worse but still I wouldn't budge.

I noticed, however, that my people were beginning to heed him. Hearing of the Seventh Plague, my people took their remaining livestock indoors, and shut their doors and windows. Some were still sceptical like me. They were outdoors when the hailstones came. Great drum rolls of thunder seemed to crack open the sky. Fire flashed out and raced along the ground in the form of blazing fireballs. And the icy hail pounded everything in sight, battering crops, shattering trees. Only in Goshen, where the wretched Hebrews lived, there was sunshine and a complete absence of hail.

'I admit it,' I said to Moses, at last. 'I must have sinned to bring this devastation on fair Egypt. Go, take your people and go!'

Moses went outside and raised his hands. Within minutes, the wind died, the hail stopped and the sun shone again. But as the wind died, so did my momentary lapse into weakness. I turned Moses away, and I waited.

A terrible wind brought the Eighth Plague out of the east. It was a tempest of locusts. They droned and whirred and settled on every inch of land and tree, and soon not a single shred of green remained throughout the whole of my incomparable land. I would have allowed Moses to take the men, if he would leave the women and children and livestock behind. But that he would not do and so the battle continued.

The Ninth Plague brought darkness. It fell like a blanket out of the sky, thick, impenetrable darkness. No light could pass through.

I couldn't see my own hand if I held it before my face! For three whole days, Egypt lay shrouded in deep and unbroken darkness, while the Hebrews basked in light.

It was insufferable! 'Leave your flocks behind and be gone!' I said to Moses. But he was as stubborn as I am, and he refused.

At midnight, I was woken by a bone-chilling cry. I threw open my palace windows and I leaned into a wall of lamentation. In every house, hut and mansion the lights were on. From every house the sound of terrible wailing pierced the cold night. My servants came running in. 'It is the worst plague of all, O Pharaoh,' they said, falling on their faces before me. 'Every house has lost its firstborn! No one is spared! Let this man take his people. His forces are mightier than ours!'

That I should live to hear such words! No Pharaoh is meant for defeat. And yet defeat was mine, bitter and galling. I called Moses and told him to take his men, women, children and cattle, every single wretched one, and leave Egypt forever. The wailing was replaced by a sound that was even more painful to my ears. It was the cheer of two million Israelites who had just been granted their freedom.

I let them leave. I sat in my golden palace and I let them all leave. It was as if I had become numbed by my own powerlessness. And then suddenly I stirred.

'Fetch the captain of the guards!' I ordered.

He arrived.

'Get the army ready at once! Put together a column of six hundred chariots and prepare the Pharaoh's royal steeds. I myself will lead our men. The Hebrews think they race to freedom, but in truth, they race towards their own deaths!'

Now, it was I who was possessed. The fury of being outsmarted by a rabble-rouser from the desert, none other than the man I had made my heir, was boiling up at last. I would cut the fleeing slaves down in their tracks. They went on foot, unarmed, unaware. I would overtake them like the wind and cut them down!

We rode faster than forked lightning. Before long, I could see a great pillar of fire. It was night and the Hebrews had camped by the Red Sea. Fools! They thought they would cross at dawn. There would be no dawn for them! They had chosen badly. The mountains lay to the south, the Red Sea before them to the east and from the west we came, an army of death.

Raising a bloodcurdling war-cry, I led my men towards the camp. I could see confusion break out in the ranks. They were not warriors, they were slaves! I could almost hear them accusing their 'saviour'. 'Why have you brought us into the wilderness to die?' they would shout. 'Even a slave's life is better than death!' Now he would know how I felt when he turned against me! He was trapped!

We were almost there. We saw him raise his rod. And then we saw something that seemed impossible. Where one unbroken expanse of water had lain, two towering walls of water had formed, leaving a strip of dry land in between. The Red Sea had parted at Moses' command! The Hebrews saw what their leader had done and at once, they ran to cross. The slaves were escaping from right under my nose!

We galloped down and plunged on to the bed of the sea. Suddenly, the pillar of fire that had been hovering over the camp blazed in front of us. We dodged it only to find ourselves riding into a column of smoke. Our horses lost their step and ran amok. Chariot wheels swerved and stuck and broke off. I was leading an army of chaos.

And still I kept my eyes fixed on the fleeing Hebrews, running across on foot, climbing the far shore, turning back to look at us, jeering and gesturing. I kept my eyes fixed on Moses. He was the last to step off the sea bed on to the shore. I saw him turn and raise his rod. He stretched out his hand and for a moment I wished I could have taken it. But he was my enemy and as I rode, I knew I was doomed.

Moses stretched out his hand and with an enormous roaring, the waters started to roll in. Behind me, I heard the cries of my drowning men.

Moses had saved his people after all. He had saved them and defeated me. I was dying and the Hebrews were speeding towards a new life.

My whole life passed before my eyes. And then, my ears were filled with the roar.

Hurry and hide,

before they catch up.

n the middle of the desert there stood a town called Mecca. It was a bustling town. Every day, camel caravans left its gates laden with silks and dates for far-off places. Every day, merchants and moneylenders counted gold into chests of burnished wood, which they kept hidden under their beds. Every day, feasts and banquets were thrown, where the rich townspeople ate off silver plates till they could hardly stand. It was Mecca the Magnificent! No one wanted to change it. Except Muhammad.

Muhammad was the only person in that whole happy town who was sad with the way things were.

'They feast and flaunt their wealth,' he thought sadly. 'They feast, and they forget!'

They were the Quraysh, and what they had forgotten was the Year of the Elephant.

That was the year the Abyssinian governor of Southern Arabia tried to invade Mecca and destroy our most holy shrine, the Kaaba. The governor was jealous of how well Mecca was doing. And so he brought an army and camped outside the gates. The soldiers rattled their spears and the drummers beat tattoos on their war drums. The sound alone made the Quraysh shiver in their shoes. Once, they had no shoes, they ranged barefoot in the desert and were grim and hardy. But now they had gone soft in the belly and timid in the soul. Mecca would fall!

And so it would have, if God hadn't intervened. Just as the army was about to attack, a plague descended on the soldiers. Unable to stand or see, the unshakeable army, horses, men, generals, the governor himself, turned and ran for their lives!

The only creature that didn't run was an elephant. It was a mammoth elephant. It stood there, implacable.

The Quraysh were feeling a lot bolder now that the army had vanished. They crept out of the city gates and cautiously approached the elephant. They had never seen such a creature before. Such flapping ears like tents, such sturdy legs like pillars, such tiny eyes like seeds, such a long curling nose like a snake and such long white teeth like curved swords! They stood at a safe distance and gaped.

The elephant, bored perhaps by the lack of action, decided to take a walk towards the city. Each step measured ten steps of a man! As they watched the elephant's hypnotic lumbering gait, it did something peculiar. It raised its curling nose, made a trumpeting sound and fell to its knees! Why on earth did it do that?

Suddenly one of the wiser Quraysh understood. The mute beast had sensed the twenty-mile sanctuary around the Kaaba where fighting was forbidden. The creature had realized it was on sacred ground! It was a harmless and wise creature after all, not a rampaging war-machine!

Next morning, they didn't feel quite so sure. The army had gathered again, ashamed of its inglorious behaviour. The elephant was on its feet and a soldier was goading it to rush at the city gates and break them down. The elephant didn't move. Suddenly, a flock of birds appeared out of nowhere, screeching and screaming, coastal birds far from their salty shores. The soldiers looked up in alarm, and before they knew it, the birds had dropped millions of pebbles on them and whirled away. The pebbles stung their unprotected arms and faces. When the soldiers looked down, they saw they were covered in horrible boils.

Soon everyone knew this story. Even the Bedouin remarked that the Quraysh were the people of God, as God Himself had saved the Quraysh.

But the Quraysh had forgotten. Swollen-headed and swagger-chested, they had a new god. Money. Every day, they performed the ritual prayers at the Kaaba, circling seven times around the sacred stone following the direction of the sun and bowing to the three hundred and sixty idols of Arabia's three hundred and sixty tribes. But the centre of their devotions was no longer God, it was their own prosperity.

It was this that Muhammad wanted to change.

'Have you forgotten who made us?' he cried to the Quraysh. 'Who made the rain pour down, and the grass grow, and loaded the palms and the olives and the vines with fruit so that we may never go hungry, and neither may our flocks? Who stopped the invaders in the Year of the Elephant? Who brought a plague on the Abyssinians that our holy shrine might be safe? Who made the summer and winter caravans go in safety and come back bearing great riches?'

But the Quraysh paid no heed. They were too busy filling their coffers and competing with one another to take Muhammad seriously.

'Even the sun and the moon and the stars bow to the Creator,' Muhammad said. 'They rise and set at his bidding. Trees bow their heads to the ebb and flow of seasons. The earth itself gives fruits and grain and herbs as thanksgiving to the God who set us on the earth to enjoy His goodness. There is a natural balance to the world, which you are trying to destroy by putting yourself above it. God has shown me the right way. We must be humble like the natural world and bow our heads in prayer towards Him who guides us all!'

But his words fell on deaf ears. The only people who listened to him were the women, the slaves and the poor people. The poor found great wealth in his words. For them, Muhammad brought a message of hope. But the rich only came to listen to Muhammad in order to mock him.

'So this is what the grandson of Abd al-Muttalib has come to!' they crowed. 'Talking to a rabble of ragged men and women, riff-raff, not one self-respecting, decent person among them! What would Abd al-Muttalib say if he saw you now!'

How could Muhammad teach the Quran (which came to him line by line, verse by verse), with the Quraysh laughing and mocking him even as he spoke? But still he persisted, and one day he took

222

his followers to the Kaaba. As he led them in ritual prayer, the onlookers voiced their opinions.

'What sort of prayer is this? Imagine us, fierce nomads, ruled over by none but ourselves, grovelling on the ground like slaves! Unthinkable!'

Muhammad had touched a raw nerve. Pride. The sight of their fellow tribesmen humbling themselves to an invisible god was too much for the proud Quraysh. Soon, the only place where it was safe to perform prayers was in secret glens outside the city.

The poor and powerless! How scared the clans were that Muhammad would lead the poor and powerless against them, the rich and influential! It wasn't till I joined him that they realized even the rich could have reason to follow him. Once I joined, I made it easier for the others.

'If Abu Bakr has joined Muhammad, so can we,' the young men of rich fathers said to one another. In fact, one of them, the boy of a leading financier came to me one day, in a state of obvious distress.

'Help me, Abu Bakr!' he said. 'I dreamt I was at the edge of a fiery pit and my father was trying to push me into it. The more I struggled, the harder he pushed. I was about to topple over when I felt two hands pulling me to safety. I opened my eyes and saw Muhammad's face and then I awoke.'

'Young man,' I said. 'Your dream says it all. Join Muhammad and you will be saved from a life of burning greed and ambition!'

And so the rich young man took courage, and joined us. Three years went by like this, Muhammad preaching, and us praying, in secret.

One day, he asked forty of the Hashim clan to join him for a meal. 'I have received a sign that I should preach openly, my brothers,' he told us. 'I beg you, join me in this meal and in the feast of learning to come!' And before any of the men could speak, Ali, his son, the youngest of us all, a starry-eyed, tangle-haired boy rushed up to declare his faith.

We were now in the open. New followers joined Muhammad every day. And new divisions started appearing in Mecca every day. Fathers disowned sons, husbands fought with wives, brother turned against brother. In this charged atmosphere, Muhammad made a startling announcement. The three goddesses al-Lat, al-Uzza and Manat were not to be worshipped any more! There was only one God and that was Allah. The Quraysh were enraged. Muhammad was not just asking them to grovel on the ground in prayer, he was asking them to give up the traditions of their forefathers! They marched off to meet Abu Talib, Muhammad's uncle and the chief of the Hashim clan.

'Control your nephew!' they said. 'He is cursing our gods and insulting our forefathers. If you cannot prevent him, hand him over to us and we will put an end to him!'

Poor Abu Talib! He loved Muhammad. He had not converted

to his teachings, but that did not mean he would hand him over to be killed by an angry mob. He decided to ignore them entirely.

But the Quraysh could not be put off so easily. They returned with a new threat. 'If you are not on our side, you are on his,' they said. 'If you continue to let him make a mockery of our old faith, we will fight you both to the death.'

It was a tough moment for Abu Talib. He called Muhammad and spoke to him. 'Give it up,' he said, gently, 'or else blood will be spilt.'

Muhammad said, 'Even if they were to put the moon in one hand and the sun in the other, in order that I give this up, I cannot. I will continue till God wins, or I will die trying.'

Abu Talib was moved by the sincerity of Muhammad's words. 'Go, do as your God tells you,' he said to Muhammad. Then, to let all of Mecca know that he was on his nephew's side, he wrote stirring verses in his support. Muhammad's other uncle, however, was not convinced. Abu Lahab denounced Muhammad as a traitor and joined his rich and powerful enemies.

Rich and powerful they may have been, but the Quraysh were powerless to hurt Muhammad as long as his clan chief protected him. So they resorted to being nasty. They taunted anyone who joined Muhammad, calling them fools. They destroyed the reputation of good citizens and physically hurt those who were weak.

Bilal, the slave of one of the chiefs who hated Muhammad, was tied up and made to lie in the hot sun for a whole day with a heavy stone on his chest. When I saw this, I stormed into the chief's house, threw down a pouch of gold and said, 'Bilal is mine from this day!'

Greedy old man that he was, he didn't bother stopping me. I untied Bilal and said, 'From today, you are a free man.' Now no one could stop Bilal from following his faith in peace!

But how many Bilals could I set free? The persecution continued, and the Quraysh never stopped harassing Muhammad. Every question they asked was a jibe, a jeer.

'If he was indeed chosen by God, where were the miracles?'

'Why had God chosen such a poor and unimportant man like him?'

'Why had He not sent an angel?'

'Why was the Quran coming to him in bits and pieces?'

Whatever he said in reply displeased them. They attacked him physically in the Kaaba and posted guards at the city gates to warn newcomers against Muhammad. But again and again, the beauty of the verses of the Quran moved people, and they believed, in spite of the Quraysh's efforts.

Finally, seeing that violence and scorn were not helping, they approached Muhammad with a new offer.

'Stop this preaching and teaching,' they said, 'and we will give you anything you ask for. Money, riches, why, we will even make you king over all the tribes of Arabia, and you can then rule Mecca with us as your loyal servants.'

But Muhammad was not swayed and the Quraysh left in humiliation. In revenge, they decided to ban trade with the clans of Hashim and al-Muttalib. We were to be left alone to starve. Some were exiled to Abyssinia. The rest were at the mercy of friends and well-wishers. Secretly, they brought us food and we survived.

After two long years, four clan leaders met at the Kaaba. 'Let us tear up the document imposing the ban!' they urged. 'Let us not starve our brothers in this manner!'

They went to get the parchment on which those in favour of the ban had signed, but to their amazement all that remained of the document was a small piece on which were written the words: *In the name of Allah.* The rest of the parchment had crumbled, eaten away by worms! Convinced that this was a sign, the ban was lifted, and our exiled brothers returned.

It should have been cause for rejoicing. But instead, sadness struck. Muhammad's wife died, and soon after, Abu Talib, Muhammad's uncle and clan chief. Muhammad was now completely defenceless. Even little boys among the Quraysh began taunting him openly and throwing dirt on him as he walked by. It was a time of great loneliness and sorrow for Muhammad. All he could do was think and hope and pray.

It was at this dark time that the miracle occurred.

Muhammad was staying with his cousin, whose house was very close to the Kaaba. One night, unable to sleep, he decided to visit the shrine and recite the Quran. That would bring him some peace. His prayers over, he decided to sleep for a while in an enclosure at the northwest corner of the Kaaba. He fell into a deep sleep. Suddenly he felt someone shaking him awake. He opened his eyes. An incandescent figure stood before him. It was the angel Gabriel.

'Come with me,' Gabriel said.

Before Muhammad could answer, he found himself being carried by the angel to where a white winged horse stood. It was a horse like no other he had ever seen. Its neck was proudly arched, its tail held high, its hooves powerful and its eyes intelligent. Its name was al-Borak or Lightning. The moment Muhammad got on, al-Borak rose into the sky with the speed of light, too fast for the human eye to catch. It rode, muscles rippling like water, mane silver in the moonlight, breathing softly as if it were not moving at all. Muhammad sat without a saddle or a bridle. The air rushed about his ears, he was thousands and thousands of feet above the ground, but he was not afraid.

At last al-Borak touched down. They had reached the holy mountain of Jerusalem!

Gabriel stood sternly by his side, as three angels brought Muhammad three different goblets. The first contained wine, the second was full of milk, and the third held water. Muhammad had to choose one. Gabriel's face gave nothing away.

Allowing instinct to guide him, Muhammad picked up the second bowl, the one with the milk, and drank it. He had chosen correctly! A great ladder appeared that seemed to reach right up into the skies. 'Climb,' Gabriel said, wordlessly.

They climbed. And they climbed. Muhammad saw all the prophets that had come before him. He saw the first of the seven heavens and the last. He saw hell. And finally, he saw a throne, where a blinding light told him he was in the presence of God himself. He lost his speech, he lost his sense of who he was, he lost everything but the vision of the One who had made the universe.

When he awoke, he was renewed and strong again. His face was luminous with the memory of what he seen.

Nothing could stop him now. He had a plan. We would leave Mecca and take refuge in the oasis town of Medina. That's how simple it was.

Medina had been more open to Muhammad's teachings than Mecca. Muhammad knew that Medina would stand by him if the Quraysh should attack. And so, in the year 622, our exodus began. Secretly, in small groups, about seventy of Muhammad's followers made the trip to Medina, careful not to arouse the suspicions of the Quraysh.

I refused to leave with the others. I wanted to stand by him, and help him as he tried to persuade more Meccans to come. We would have lingered longer, if Muhammad's last remaining protector, a chief by the name of Mu'tim hadn't died. It would be unsafe to stay even one more day. We decided to leave early next morning.

But that night, I found myself being woken up by Muhammad.

'We must leave by the back door now, while it is still dark,' he said. 'Gabriel came to me and warned me. Come!'

Before we slipped out, I peered to the front of the house to see what danger we were being warned against. Bunched in the shadows was a group of young men. Killers, sent by the clan chiefs! Why hadn't they burst in and killed us already? And then I understood. The women of the house were chanting their prayers. The men had been ashamed at the idea of killing Muhammad in the presence of women! They would wait till dawn streaked the sky red and then spill blood on the cobbles as Muhammad stepped out into the street! The thought made me shudder and I turned away. We didn't have long before they found out their mistake. Next morning, when Ali would step out of the front door, dressed in his father's robes, they would send search parties after us. We had better hurry, and hide, before they caught up.

We found a cave in the mountains outside the city. We hid ourselves and waited. After three days, the first band of men could be heard coming our way.

'And what will you do with the hundred she-camels if you find Muhammad?' I heard one of them say, in an amused tone. 'Marry them?'

Coarse laughter obscured the reply. The Quraysh had obviously offered a reward of a hundred she-camels to the man who brought Muhammad back. The cave we were hiding in was small but it went in a long way. I signalled Muhammad to creep in as far back as he could. I remained where I was, crouched in the shadow of a rock just behind the entrance. The voices became clearer. They were climbing up.

'See that cave!' a young voice suddenly shouted excitedly. 'He could be in that one! Come on, let's search it!'

'Are you blind, or just stupid?' said the older voice I had heard earlier, still amused. 'Can't you see no one could have entered that cave unless he were a ghost?'

The men laughed.

'What do you mean?' the young voice said, clearly offended. 'I can see as well as any other man!'

'Well then, as I thought, you're stupid! You see the signs but do not see the meaning. What do you see at the mouth of the cave then, with your ever-so-keen eyes?'

'A spider's web,' the young man answered, grudgingly.

'Yes, but intact! If anyone had passed in the last few days it would have been broken—such an enormous web takes time to make, even for the busiest spider!'

The men laughed some more.

'And, my bright young boy, do you see the acacia tree in front of it? And at its foot a rock, exactly where you would have to put your foot to climb up to the cave?'

'Yes, what of it?' the young man snapped.

'A nest, bright boy, a rock-dove's nest and there she sits, guarding her eggs as if she has been sitting there for all time! How could anyone have climbed up without upsetting that nest, pray?'

There was no answer, and with a huge guffaw of laughter, the band of men moved on. I looked back. My amazement was reflected in Muhammad's face. None of these things had been there when we found the cave. The rock that hid me prevented my seeing what the men were talking about.

When the horses could no longer be heard, we crept to the front of the cave. It was miraculous. A shining web covered the entrance like a delicate curtain and beyond it, we saw the acacia tree that had sprung up overnight and the nest with the bird sitting on it.

'Allah looks after His own,' I said, and we offered our heartfelt thanks.

It wasn't long before the searchers gave up. We mounted the camels that had been secretly arranged for us, and began to find our way down the precarious mountainside. It was a long and circuitous journey. We couldn't travel openly, so we took the most winding and hidden paths, often turned back by rock falls and dead ends.

At last, one blue-skied September morning, we reached Quba,

at the southernmost point of Medina. Suddenly, the bare rocks were echoing with the cry: 'Here he comes!'

A crowd of men, women and children ran out to meet us. All these months they had been waiting, scanning the horizon for the Prophet and now at last he was here. Many begged him to get down and stay with them, but he went on till his camel fell to her knees outside a date shop owned by two orphan brothers. Muhammad decided that would be the spot for the mosque he would build to thank and honour his God. His flight to freedom was over. His long walk to building a new community had just begun.

THE MIRACLE
WORKER

Five loaves

and two little fish!
It was

hopeless.

y name doesn't matter. What matters is that I was there. I saw it with my own eyes. It was *my* basket he asked for, and so kindly too. Lord knows how he spotted me in that pressing crowd. But what am I saying? He was the Lord himself. He saw things no one else did.

We had followed him all the way from Jerusalem. Him and the other twelve. But it was him our eyes were fixed on, as if on a star that would never dip or die.

My baby sister had been born ill. No one had been able to cure her. Not doctors, not preachers, not charlatans. My mother's eyes watered as we walked behind him, hurrying so as not to be too late. Please please please, her lips shaped as she walked. Her arms held my tiny sister, too tiny for her age, too sick. Hurry hurry hurry, my father's eyes urged, as he walked by her side. Only I walked without muttering or thinking anything. On my head was the basket. I was careful not to let it drop.

It had started only that morning.

'Did you hear?' the old lady who walked behind us said to her neighbour, a woman more bent, more ancient than herself.

'Course I did,' the old crone replied. 'But no harm hearing it again! It was at Bethesda, was it not?'

'It was at Bethesda,' said the first, who seemed a bit hard of hearing. 'I'm surprised you haven't heard. Today the angel was to come and stir the waters. I was there myself, waiting, waiting. All the five porticoes were full. What wretches we all were! Some blind, some lame, some too old or too sick to move. Groaning, sitting, lying on the steps, waiting.'

'Yes, waiting,' the crone murmured.

'Next to me was the man who has come there every single year the last eight and thirty years. Do you know him?'

'Course I do!' the crone said. 'Who doesn't!'

'I'm surprised you don't know him,' the first one said, her voice all breathy with walking and talking. 'He's been ill these last eight and thirty years, and every year he comes, hoping the angel of the waters will cure him, and still he returns, uncured. He was lying next to where I sat when *He* came up. His face, ah, his face! So full of pity, brimming, like the pool.

'"What ails you?" he asked.

'"I haven't walked a single step these thirty-eight years," came the answer. "But this year, I hope to. My only worry is I may not reach the water in time. Everyone wants to be the first in! Someone has to lift me up and carry me into the pool. But who will? Without help, I don't have a chance. Will you give me a hand, kind sir?"

'"I won't need to," the kind sir replied. "You'll be able to walk on your own. Get up and see!"

'The words were so strange that *I* got up to see what he meant. The poor man was too afraid to even raise himself, forget stand! But the look on *His* face gave him strength I think. On his side, on his

239

elbow, on his knees and then, like a child afraid to fall, on his shaky shivering legs! He stood! I tell you, I near fainted myself. Standing after eight and thirty years! One step, two steps, then *walking*!'

The poor old woman became so keyed up she went into a fit of coughing. The other ancient mumbled along, sympathetic. Mother's eyes glittered painfully. She had so much hope, so much.

'And then when I turned around to ask the miracle-worker's name, he was gone! One moment, as real as you or me, the next moment gone! "Who made you well, who, tell us, tell us!" All us poor souls crowding around the healed man, and he not having any answer! It was like nothing I've ever seen, and me as old as the hills!'

That was how it started, truly. It seems the cured man went to the temple to give thanks, and there he met the man who healed him, and this time he asked his name. Jesus, the man said. 'My name is Jesus.'

Soon that name was flying around Jerusalem, down the steps of Bethesda, up the narrow crowded alleys, into the darkest, saddest corners. 'A man called Jesus is healing the sick! Hurry!'

And they all came pouring out, my family and I among them. He had left the city by the time we were ready with our bundle and basket and baby sister in Mother's arms.

'He leaves for Tiberias, on the other side of the Sea of Galilee!' frantic word arrived. 'He is mourning the death of John the Baptist who has been beheaded by the Roman king! His twelve disciples walk with him, the ones who brought this sorry news. And now he grieves so much, he leaves Jerusalem. Hurry, if you want to be cured!'

And so we ran. Or shuffled and stumbled and hobbled, more like it. First, it was a handful, then a hundred, then a few hundreds, then a thousand. Soon there were a few thousand of us, men, women, tiny babes, children, hurrying, being carried, limping to catch up with the man they called Jesus, and his twelve.

I had heard of the twelve before. They moved around the country spreading God's word, healing the sick and casting out demons. You couldn't tell by looking at them. Such rough tunics, like ours. Nothing in their hands except a staff, like ours. They carried no food, no money, I had heard. Some welcomed them. Some cursed and turned them away. And still they carried on, doing good where it was to be done. I admired the twelve.

I walked faster to see them a bit closer. I was so close now I could see the dust at the edge of their robes and the lines in their hardened feet. I could also hear one of them say, 'Master, you wish to be alone. Shall we send them away?'

Oh no. Would he? Oh my poor mother, if he did!

'No,' I heard him say, so softly it was like a sigh. 'No, let them come.'

We were almost near a mountain. We climbed it. My basket, which I had hardly noticed before, seemed heavy. When would we eat, I thought. Who knows how long we will walk before he stops. I felt hungry. I stopped to let my family catch up with me. The others pressed on ahead. Mother was tired, I could see. My baby sister looked like a bundle of rags, hardly moving.

And then he stopped. We had reached the top of the mountain. He turned to face us. He was tired, as tired as Mother, as sorrowful. More. Suddenly, I felt we should all go away and let him be alone, he looked that sad and that troubled. He looked at us long and hard. All the talking muttering whispering wheezing died down. I heard a bird sing one clear note. And then he smiled and said, 'Come.'

It was like watching the sun break through a mass of heavy cloud! One by one, we went forward, and one by one, he healed us all. Mother trembled so she could hardly hold my baby sister up. Father had to do it. Jesus placed his hand on her brow and she was well. A rosy pink filled her cheeks, the grey sickness vanished and my sister was well again. So were the others. Women wept with joy. Crippled children ran around, laughing. Parents held each other's hands. I stole a look at the miracle-worker. His own grief had lifted. His brow was lined, but he was less sad, seeing how happy he had made us all. So happy, that we hadn't noticed how late it was.

The sun had gone down, a chill wind crept under our robes and made us shiver. I felt ravenous. But how were we to eat our food, surrounded by so many who might have forgotten to bring their own? And so I hushed up and fought the thought of food.

It was then that one of the twelve came up to me, directly, without searching, as if he had always known me.

'The master wants to speak to you,' he said. 'No, don't put it down, bring it along.'

I was so surprised I went without a word. Mother was too absorbed in kissing Sister's rosy cheeks to notice.

'Do you mind if we share your food with the crowd?' the master of the twelve asked me, gently.

I gasped.

'O no, sir, master, no not at all, but . . .' I babbled I was so nervous.

'Speak without fear, young man,' said the kindly one who had fetched me.

'It will not be enough, sir, master,' I blurted out. 'Only five barley loaves we packed and two fish. We didn't . . .'

One of the twelve burst out, 'How can five barley loaves and two fish be of any use! Look at the size of this crowd! I still say we should send them back home.'

I turned red. I knew my basket would be of no use, and I felt a fool just standing there, as if it would.

Another of the twelve said, worriedly this time, 'We do not even have enough money to buy bread to feed them! Only two hundred denarii among the twelve of us!'

I looked from one to the other. What should I do? Then the master of the twelve spoke again.

'If you do not mind, young man,' he said to me, 'put down your basket and let us see what we can do.'

Feeling all their eyes on me, I put down the basket.

'Open it,' the doubting one said.

I opened it. I hadn't lied. Five barley loaves and two fish were all that lay inside my wicker basket. It was hopeless. The twelve murmured worriedly.

But the master of the twelve said, 'Tell them to sit down on the grass.'

I could feel their doubt hanging in the air as they went to do their master's bidding. They walked among the crowd, making the people sit in groups of fifty and hundred each. If possible, the people seemed even happier now, in the almost-dark. I could sense it. After days, maybe years, they were happy again, and with happiness came the keenness of hunger. And now it seemed as if their Healer was making this wish come true as well! Food, shared with the master, on the mountain top! I could sense their expectation growing. I stood where I was, stiff, by the open basket, wondering.

Five loaves and two little fish! Barely enough for the four of us, and Mother who ate so little and Sister but a baby! I could see my worry on the faces of the twelve as they walked back, unsure.

But the master was sure. He raised the food towards heaven and blessed it. Then he broke the bread, gave it to his disciples and said, 'Go and feed the people.'

The twelve did as they were told. The kind one beckoned me to help them. I rushed forward. We went from group to group. I carried the basket and they broke the loaves and placed pieces of fish into waiting hands.

The first group of fifty gratefully received handfuls of bread and fish. I looked into the basket. It looked fuller than when we had started! I caught the twelve exchanging secret looks. I felt the same. Is this possible? Are we imagining it?

But as we moved from group to group, the basket in my arms never emptied. No matter how large the hunks of bread or how generous the helpings of fish. The twelve looked entranced. I know I did too.

Unaware of the miracle that was happening before their eyes, the people ate their fill. The bread was soft and the fish delicious. Children asked for more and old men who had not felt like eating for months relished every toothless bite they took. One thought united them all—this was the best feast they ever had!

Once everyone had been served, we ate, me sitting shyly at the side of the twelve and their master. Then the master said, 'Go and collect what has been left over. Food this good must not be wasted.'

What could be left? I was surprised, once again. My basket was not enough. We took twelve empty baskets and we filled them all! Five thousand men, women and children had eaten heartily from five barley loaves and two fish, and still there was more to spare!

In the early morning, when I woke, the twelve and their master had gone. They had much work to do, and places to go, and people to heal. I took Mother's hand, and we walked home. The master hadn't just filled our bellies. He had filled our hearts, and we were content.

But the magic vessel is empty!

had got used to living in exile. True, it wasn't the kind of life I had imagined for myself as a young girl. And never after marrying the five brothers did I think that one day I might come to this! But it was my fate, and I had sworn to walk every road with them. Finally, one of those roads would lead back to Hastinapura and our rightful kingdom. Finally, Yudhishthira would win back what he had staked so recklessly over a throw of dice. How I hated those dice! He lost his reason when he saw them tumble on to that treacherous board! And so he lost everything—our kingdom, our home, our wealth . . . and our dignity. Never for a second could I forget the shame of being dragged out like that by my hair, while my five great and good husbands sat by, mute and helpless. If Krishna hadn't saved me then, I don't know what I would have done. I knew, till I was avenged for that wrong I would never rest!

But till then, I would share this meagre life with my husbands. At least, the gods had not deserted us. One day, right at the beginning of our life in the forest, when I was wondering what kind of meals could be made out of herbs and berries, the Sun God appeared before me.

'Take this vessel, Draupadi,' he said. 'It will give you unlimited quantities of food once a day, but only till you yourself have eaten! Once you have eaten, it will remain empty till the next day. Use it wisely, and you and yours will never go hungry!'

And the Sun God had disappeared, leaving that magic vessel in my wondering hands. It worked just as he said. Knowing that the

248

Pandavas had settled in that part of the country, countless *munis* and Brahmins started to visit. I would have died if I hadn't had that vessel! They arrived, I fed them, and only after every last one had been satisfied did I sit down and eat. And then, just as the Sun God said, the vessel yielded not even a single morsel until the next sunrise. It was incredible.

Forest life was not so bad, really. I would sit for hours watching the skip and slide of light on the river as it murmured over the flat white stones. I would be awakened by birdsong and go to sleep on grass beds so soft I hardly remembered where I was.

In fact, it was about time for me to take my afternoon rest. It had been a quiet day, just my husbands and I, and after scouring out the vessel, I prepared to lie down. That was when disaster struck.

I heard Yudhishthira addressing someone.

'Welcome, O sage,' he said, in his most courteous manner. 'It is a great honour to have you visit us here, in the forest! You must allow us to serve you. Once you and your revered companions have had your bath in the river, join us for a feast. It is the least we can do to celebrate your coming!'

A feast! My heart quaked. For whom? And how? Peeping outside, I saw a sight that made my stomach feel hollow, even though I had just eaten. It was the sage Durvasa, with his matted locks and knotted eyebrows! He was known for his terrible temper. Even the smallest mistake was enough to bring on his wrath! And he was not alone. Behind him stood ten thousand of his disciples, all of whom my husband had so sweetly invited for lunch! But what else could he have done? The slightest discourtesy would mean one of sage Durvasa's famous curses.

Yudhishthira probably had no idea that I had already eaten. The magic vessel would be useless till the next morning. What was I to do now? And how was it that sage Durvasa had arrived without warning that day of all days, at the very minute that I had finished eating?

. . .

The answer to Draupadi's questions lay far away in Hastinapura. King Dhritarashtra's son Duryodhana had received news that made him most displeased. Having got his cousins, the Pandavas, exiled to the forest for twelve years, he had begun to consider himself the happiest man in the world. Surely the princes and their delicate wife Draupadi would not survive the long years of hardship!

And even if by some miracle they managed to, they would certainly be discovered during the thirteenth year that they were supposed to spend in disguise. It was impossible that they should remain successfully hidden! Yudhishthira with his clear and truthful gaze, Arjuna with his warrior stance, Bhima with his mighty arms, Nakula and Sahadeva with their winsome looks. And Draupadi, the dark-eyed one, who had mocked him! There was no one who wouldn't recognize them! Come to think of it, there was no one who didn't sing their praises behind his back, even now, after they had been stripped of their wealth and glory. He hated them all, and he was counting on the fact that someone would see through their disguises and so condemn them to twelve more years in the forest. It had seemed a foolproof plan then, but the news that came to him now worried him more than he cared to show.

'It seems that the Pandavas are enjoying their exile, O Duryodhana!' the messengers said to him. 'They are not lacking for food or for company. It seems that the Sun God himself has given Draupadi a miraculous vessel that produces unlimited quantities of food! Till she herself eats, the vessel brims over with the most delicious and strengthening offerings! And as for company, why, *munis* from all over seek them out and spend hours with them in the shade of the trees, talking of everything under the sun. Ascetics and sages visit them all the time, for news of their generosity has spread far and wide. It seems, O Duryodhana, as if Yudhishthira is holding court even in the forest!'

'This is intolerable!' Duryodhana exploded, after the messengers had gone, and he was alone with his brother Dushasana and his closest friend Karna. 'Something must be done. Think, for we must not allow them to spite us even from afar!'

The three of them racked their brains, but they couldn't come up with anything that seemed harmful enough. It was around this time that sage Durvasa happened to arrive in Hastinapura with his ten thousand disciples. Duryodhana received them with great humility and waited on the great *muni* himself. At any hour of the day or night, he stood ready to please Durvasa's smallest whim.

The sage was as unpredictable as everyone said he was. Sometimes he would be in a tearing hurry. 'Feed us at once!' he would command. It would be done. Sometimes he would give the summons for food to be served and then go off to bathe. Coming back hours later, he would brush Duryodhana off, saying, 'I am not hungry any longer,' and disappear. Sometimes, as if to test Duryodhana's patience, he would wake up in the middle of the night and ask for a complete meal. The minute the meal was ready he would yawn, turn over in his bed and go right back to sleep! This went on for quite some time. No matter how hard he pushed Duryodhana or how unreasonable his demands, Duryodhana stayed calm and sweet-tempered.

This good behaviour did not escape the keen eyes of the irascible old man. One day, he said to Duryodhana, 'I am pleased with your attentions, my son. Your irreproachable conduct has earned you a boon. Ask me for anything that is not irreligious or immoral, and it shall be yours!'

These words were like music to Duryodhana's ears! All these days, he had swallowed his pride and remained humble and patient hoping for just such a moment. In fact, Karna, Dushasana and he had already decided what to ask for if the sage should feel mellow enough to grant them a boon. And so, without hesitation, bowing very low so that Durvasa could not see the flicker of unholy excitement in his eyes, Duryodhana said, 'O great sage, you are very kind! Just having you amongst us is boon enough for me. But since you heap honour upon honour, I have just one favour to ask. Not for myself, but for my brother Yudhishthira, who is the eldest and best of our race. As you know, he lives with his pure-souled brothers and his virtuous wife in the forest. I beg you, be his guest for some time just as you have been mine. Nothing could please me more. Arrive at his ashram just as Draupadi, having fed the Brahmins, her husbands and herself, lies down to rest. Only this I ask, in all humility!'

It was an oily speech, falsehood cloaked in fake sincerity. But sage Durvasa, having given his word, agreed. Duryodhana, Dushasana and Karna were filled with glee. Their plan had worked! The Pandavas would incur the scorching wrath of sage Durvasa and that would be the end of them! They saw the sage off, and Durvasa went on till he arrived in the forest where the Pandavas lived.

. . .

For some minutes I remained frozen to the spot. I was aghast at the prospect of turning away the great sage, unfed. And then, suddenly, there I was on my knees, praying.

'Krishna, help me!' I said, urgently, under my breath. 'Once before I have called on you and you came! Save me again, O Lord of the universe, bringer of all good, refuge of the helpless. O blue-skinned, yellow-robed Vasudeva, my friend, my saviour, come to my aid now!'

I could see him in my mind's eye, far away in Dwarka, but never too far away to be deaf to my entreaty. I could see his kind face, the priceless gem shining at his breast, his merry eyes . . .

'Well, aren't you going to get up and greet me? Or are you just going to sit there staring?'

He was standing in front of me, in the hut!

'You've come!' I said, not believing my eyes and yet knowing it was true. 'I knew you would! I'm in trouble . . . listen!'

And I told him about the arrival of sage Durvasa with his ten thousand disciples. '. . . and just after I'd finished eating! Now there's not a morsel to be had! What will I do? If he goes hungry I can't even imagine what he will do. Probably wipe us all out! Don't smile, do something!'

I was frantic. But Krishna didn't seem to care. He just heard me out and then said, 'That reminds me—I haven't had my midday meal either. Get me some food first, Draupadi, and then you can think about the others!'

'What?' I exclaimed. 'Haven't you been listening? I've already eaten my meal! The vessel will remain empty till tomorrow. Don't tease me now, Krishna, not when I'm almost faint with worry!'

'Who's teasing who?' Krishna laughed. 'Here am *I* almost faint with hunger and you just stand there, talking. Get me the vessel, quick!'

What was he playing at? I didn't know whether to be puzzled, anxious or just plain angry. Still, he was Krishna, my friend and saviour, and he had never let me down.

I went and brought the magic vessel. He looked into it and said, 'See, I knew you were fooling me! It's not empty—there's a tiny bit of rice and spinach sticking to its side!' And picking out the tiny morsel, he popped it into his mouth. 'May Lord Hari, the soul of the universe, be satisfied with this morsel!' he said. Then he turned around to me and said, 'What are you gaping at? Go tell Bhima to call the *munis* to their meal!'

'What? But . . .' It made absolutely no sense. True, there had been a morsel left, but how would that feed ten thousand and one hungry stomachs? Besides, even that morsel was no longer there!

Completely at a loss, I went out and told Bhima to fetch the sage and his *munis*. I didn't tell Yudhishthira that I had already eaten. What was the use? Either we would be saved, or wrath would descend. I wanted to wait a while and see. At least, till Bhima returned. By then, surely something would happen.

. . .

Down by the river, the *munis* had almost finished bathing. They had all been looking forward to a good meal, and that made them hurry. But as they came out of the water, a peculiar thing happened. All ten thousand of them began feeling very full, as if they had just eaten at a feast. They approached the sage hesitantly.

'We are worried, master,' they said. 'We have told Yudhishthira to prepare our meal, but suddenly we do not feel in the least hungry! How will we eat when our stomachs are already so full?'

The sage was feeling exactly the same way. He looked troubled.

'There is only one way out then,' he said. 'We must leave at once. By refusing the feast that the good Yudhishthira must undoubtedly have prepared for us by now, we will be doing him a great wrong. He is blessed by Hari himself, and an insult such as this might spark off a wrath far greater than mine! We cannot go back, we must travel on.'

And so, sage Durvasa and his ten thousand disciples left the forest as suddenly as they had arrived.

Duryodhana's wicked plan had just been foiled.

. . .

Where was Bhima? Why did he take so long? I felt anxious and impatient. Yudhishthira noticed that something was bothering me.

'Why do you fret?' he asked gently, sitting down next to me. 'The Sun God's magic vessel has never failed us before. Even sage Durvasa will be happy with its offerings.'

I couldn't bear it any more. I blurted it out. 'But the magic vessel is empty! I had already eaten when you invited the sage to stay!'

Yudhishthira's face fell.

Just then Bhima came racing up, panting.

'I cannot find them anywhere!' he gasped. 'I looked up and

down the river, at all the bathing places, and not one *muni* did I see!
They have vanished!'

'Perhaps we have angered him somehow,' Yudhishthira said,
sombrely. 'If it was anyone else I would be relieved, now that I know
there *is* no meal to be had. But sage Durvasa! No good can come of
sage Durvasa going away unfed from our door!'

And he told his brothers of the magic vessel being empty. My
husbands were plunged into gloom.

'What if they come back at night?' Nakula said suddenly. 'The
sage might be wanting to test us!'

I hadn't thought of that. My dejection deepened. I had almost
forgotten . . . Krishna. Krishna stepped out of the hut.

'What are you mourning, faces all long and shoulders all
drooping?' he said, gaily. 'These miserable creatures aren't the
Pandavas I knew! Come on, cheer up.'

My dejection vanished, swift as mist in the morning sun. It was
inexplicable.

'Stop worrying! It is I who sent the rishi and his disciples away!
Naturally, once Draupadi had fed them, they felt no need to return!'

My husbands looked at me. I probably looked more surprised
than they did. We turned, as one, towards Krishna, hoping he
would explain.

'Don't ask me, ask her!' he laughed, tossing his head towards
me. 'If she hadn't called me, I wouldn't have come, and if I hadn't

come, I wouldn't have had that delicious morsel of rice and spinach, and if I hadn't eaten that morsel, the sage and his men wouldn't have felt so full . . .'

'And if they hadn't felt so full, they wouldn't have run away!' Arjuna completed, excitedly. 'There were afraid to insult us by refusing our feast, so they fled! Wonderful!'

'The feast that wasn't there!' said Nakula, beginning to laugh like a boy.

'And you sent me all the way to look for them, knowing they weren't there in the first place!' Bhima complained. 'And made me hungry all over again! How about filling *my* stomach this time?'

My husbands burst out laughing. Krishna joined them, looking utterly delighted with himself.

'What if they return tonight?' I asked.

'Not tonight, nor any other day!' Krishna said. 'You can all live in peace!'

He had done it again. He had saved me and my family from disaster and disgrace. I fell to my knees and thanked him. My husbands, whose laughter merely hid their deep thankfulness and wonder, did the same. He blessed us, the blue-skinned, yellow-robed one, and returned to Dwarka.

And not for a day did I forget how Lord Krishna, my friend, my saviour, made one grain of rice satisfy the hunger of ten thousand disciples and one formidable sage.

THE HEROIC
CHILD

What sort of **enemy** was hiding in this **skinny young** boy?

eople say my father was an evil man. I wouldn't go that far. In fact, he wasn't a man at all. He was a demon. Actually, that's not true either. He was the king of the demons. And by the time I come into the story, even that description wouldn't be strictly accurate. You see, by then, he had become the king of all three worlds. Men feared him. Gods didn't dare get in his way. And as for the poor demons, they simply quaked each time my father even *looked* in their direction. Now do you begin to see why everyone hated him so? He was too powerful, too big, too strong. As for me, I didn't hate him. He was my father after all, even if he *did* try to kill me. You see, I was luckier than he was. He had no friends. Slaves, yes. But friends, no. Whereas I . . .

But wait. I'm telling this all wrong. Let me start at the beginning.

My name is Prahlad. My father's name is Hiranyakashipu. He lived thousands and thousands of years ago when people could get what they wanted by doing terribly difficult things called penances. My father, who wanted to be the king of all three worlds, chose the most difficult penance of all.

In his hermitage, high above the mountains, he stood on one toe, arms raised high above his head, his eyes fixed on the immense blue sky. He stood like this for days and nights without number. The sun burned him, the winds buffeted him, the rains soaked him and the snows froze him stiff. Still he stood, season after season, straight and unwavering, not noticing the numbness in his limbs and the weakness in his bones. In fact, his concentration was so great and his penance so intense, that it had to explode in some way.

One day, it did. A great fire burst out of his head and spread in all four directions. The fire blazed as wildly as the light in my father's eyes, and spread as uncontrollably as his wish to be the most powerful king of all. The gods, who were sitting peacefully in heaven, suddenly found themselves choking and coughing as great puffs of smoke crept into their nostrils and huge licks of flame flickered at their feet and scorched their faces. Leaving their seats in a hurry, they rushed to Brahmalok, where the Creator of all things, Lord Brahma himself, sat.

'Save us, O Brahma!' they begged. 'The Daitya king Hiranyakashipu's penance is turning all the three worlds to ash! It must be stopped, and only you can stop him!'

Brahma knew it was time for him to act. Accompanied by his wise men, he went at once to my father's hermitage. The wise men, it is said, were furious when they saw that my father made no attempt to bow down to Brahma. He just stood there, lost in his penance.

Lord Brahma spoke. 'Break your concentration, Hiranyakashipu!' he said. 'I have been greatly impressed by your penance. You deserve a boon. Choose it, and it's yours.'

My father didn't hesitate. 'Lord of all creatures,' he said. 'Grant that I may never be killed! Not by man, and not by beasts. Not by gods, demons or seers. Not in fact, by any of the beings in nature.'

'Done,' Lord Brahma said.

But my father had not finished. 'Not by weapons, O Brahma, and not by one of your wondrous thunderbolts. Not inside my house, nor outside it. Not in heaven, nor on earth, not by night nor by day, not from above nor from below!'

The wise men looked at each other and raised their eyebrows. Wasn't my father asking for too much? But even if he was, what could they do? And if Lord Brahma didn't seem worried, who were they to object?

And sure enough, there was Lord Brahma granting my father his heart's dearest wish. 'It shall be just as you asked,' he said. 'Now stop your penance and return to your duties.'

Music to his ears! My father lowered his arms at last and placed both feet on the ground. Everything creaked and ached. His stomach had caved in and his flesh had fallen away. But what did he care! He joined his withered hands and thanked Lord Brahma. And then he walked away, free at last to do as he pleased.

Which meant that things got pretty unpleasant for anyone who opposed him. Wearing his invincibility like a suit of armour, my father started waging war against the gods. Appalled by his cheek but unable to do a thing about it, the gods soon found themselves forced out of the heavens. Displaced and fuming, they wandered about the earth, disguised as men.

But that didn't help much. Soon, my father had taken over the kingdoms of men as well. Mortal kings and their subjects were now under his thumb. There was no escaping it. Hiranyakashipu, King of the Daityas, my father, was now officially King of All Three Worlds. He sent out an official proclamation.

FROM THIS DAY ON, I, HIRANYAKASHIPU, AM SOLE AND SOVEREIGN MASTER OF ALL THREE WORLDS. GODS, MEN AND DEMONS SHALL BOW DOWN BEFORE ME. IN TEMPLES, SHRINES AND HOMES, NO ONE SHALL BE WORSHIPPED BUT ME. ALL SACRIFICES AND OFFERINGS SHALL BE MADE TO ME AND ME ALONE. LET NO ONE FORGET THIS. ANYONE WHO BREAKS THIS LAW SHALL MEET THE SEVEREST PUNISHMENT. DEATH.

I admit, it was strong stuff. Not the kind of thing that makes you an instant favourite. But who was to tell my father that? He sat, glittering coldly in his splendid crystal palace, unapproachable, served by Gandharvas and Siddhas, and entertained by divinely beautiful apsaras who normally danced only for the gods. Hiranyakashipu's name spelt terror. No one dared go against him.

Except me.

The funny thing was, the last thing I wanted to do was go against him. I didn't want to fight. I didn't know how. Besides, how could I? I was a frail boy, no muscles to speak of, absolutely hopeless. I was probably a great disappointment to my father. How he must have wished I was big and brawny like him! How he must have wanted me to excel at wrestling and archery and sword-fights! But I was no good at any of those. And still I went into battle. Or rather, my father went into battle with me.

I never suspected what it would lead to the day my father asked me what I had been learning. You see, he had sent me off to live with a Brahmin teacher, away from the distractions of the court. I was very happy studying. Books delighted me the way games delighted other boys. Some time after my father had settled down as undisputed master, he sent for me.

'Well boy,' he said, in his usual gruff way. 'What have you learnt?'

It was a tricky question. Where would I start? I had been taught lots of things, but what had I truly learnt? Only one answer seemed to cover the whole range of emotions I felt when my father asked me that seemingly simple question.

'To adore Vishnu, Father,' I said, softly.

'What?'

I looked up. My father had turned purple with rage. I could tell what was passing through his mind. The inhabitants of all three worlds swore they adored only him, and here was his stripling son saying he adored Vishnu! He turned on my teacher and accused him of the crime of disobeying the great sovereign's commands.

'No Father,' I said, quickly. 'It's not his fault. He hasn't broken your laws. My teacher is Vishnu himself, and how can you blame Vishnu? He is, after all, the teacher of the whole universe and the protector of us all, even you!'

I had gone too far.

'Blasphemy!' my father shouted. 'You are possessed by an evil spirit!'

'No Father,' I said. 'Only by Vishnu.'

'Take him away!' my father shouted. His slaves rushed forward. 'And don't you dare utter such nonsense again!'

I went away.

It wasn't long before another visit was due. I don't know which of us was more nervous, my father, or I. After hemming and hawing a bit, my father asked me to sing a song. Since I had already disgraced him once by speaking, he probably thought a song was a safer idea. I didn't have a problem with that. I sang. It was one of my favourite songs. I know I sang it well. It was a hymn in praise of Vishnu. It flowed off my tongue and rang through the court. At least this time, I hoped my father would be pleased.

I was wrong. I looked at him after the last verse got over. His face was like thunder. I had offended him publicly, again. My heart shook but I didn't look away.

'Seize the boy and kill him!'

I had trouble believing my ears. What was my father saying? Was I dreaming?

One look at the hordes of demons descending on me and I

knew this was no dream. It was real. Their weapons were horrifying. Sharp, curved and twisted steel. Spiked, poisoned and deadly steel. Even a hardened warrior would have fainted at the sight. I was as good as dead.

But something held me up. Some strong force, which I had never felt before, resisted the rush of metal, and I found myself speaking calmly.

'Vishnu is in your weapons, just as He is in me. You cannot hurt me.'

And as if just speaking the words out loud made them true, the demons couldn't hurt me. They struck again and again, but I didn't feel a thing. Not a cut appeared, not a wound.

My father was more flabbergasted than the soldiers.

'Forget about Vishnu,' he blustered. 'Or else you will come to more harm than you can possibly imagine.'

'I won't, Father,' I found myself saying. 'I have a friend who will save me, no matter what you do.' For I had just discovered where my strength came from, and it made me braver than I had ever felt before.

What for me was a great discovery, for my father was a great insult. He whom the gods had not been able to stop was being threatened by some invisible friend of his puny son!

He summoned the snake deities and ordered them to bite me. They struck their venomous fangs against my foot, and their fangs broke. They darted and struck and hissed and lashed about with frustration, failing to bite me even once. My teacher, who was there, looking on in horror, told me that all the time the snakes lashed and writhed about, I just stood there quietly, as if watching a river flow past my ankles.

As the snakes fell away, harmless as vines, my father shouted, 'O elephants of the skies, come down and gore my wilful son to death!'

The elephants obeyed. Each was enormous, with even more enormous tusks. They stood shoulder to shoulder, a mighty grey wall, and then they charged.

It was as if a mountain had fallen. I really cannot tell how I withstood that charge. But it seems I did, for before I knew it, the Daityas in the court were shouting and the elephants were lying on their sides, their tusks blunt and useless.

My father was not impressed. In fact, he was getting madder by the minute. His thoughts were clear to see. What was the force in his son that resisted such incredible violence? What sort of enemy was hiding in this skinny young boy with bare shoulders and empty hands? His rage at his unseen enemy was so great that he became blind to the fact that he was trying to destroy me, his own son. To him, I was no longer Prahlad, but a deadly foe who needed to be wiped out.

'Build a fire around him!' he ordered. Great piles of firewood were brought and stacked in a circle around me. The fire was lit.

'O Wind God, fan the flames with your breath!' he ordered. The Wind God had no option but to obey. He sent a strong breeze that made the wood catch fire instantly. I was in a well of flame. But why did it feel so pleasant? And what was that lovely smell?

'Father!' I called out. 'Come in and stand here beside me. It is so cool and pleasant and I can smell flowers—yes, lotuses!'

Though I couldn't see him, I knew my father would be tearing his hair in anger.

'Use sorcery if you must,' I heard him say, 'but destroy him!'

The fire died down and I found myself facing a terrifying female apparition. She had a flaming trident in her hand, and she stepped forward and struck me on the chest with it. The crowd gasped. The trident shattered into a hundred pieces and the evil force aimed at me doubled back and consumed the court priests who had conjured it up.

I felt terrible. The priests were simply following my father's orders. That was no reason for them to die.

'Please God,' I found myself whispering. 'Please Lord Vishnu! Bring them back to life.'

The gasp that followed made me open my eyes. The priests had reappeared, all of them, and to my great embarrassment, they fell at my feet and thanked me.

'I didn't do it,' I whispered to them, deliriously happy. 'Lord Vishnu did!'

'Where do you get this magic from?' my father bellowed, above the tumult in the court.

'Simply from not wishing any harm to anyone, Father,' I said. I had wanted to say from Vishnu, but I knew that would only enrage him further. But this answer seemed bad enough. Not wishing any harm to anyone was no way to become powerful, my father thought. This was the worst kind of mockery!

'Take him to the top of the palace walls and fling him down!' he said. 'That might put some sense into him, even if it kills him!'

The sentries grabbed me and carried me up. I could have easily walked up on my own, but no, they were afraid I would run away.

I knew the palace ramparts well. My father had sealed himself into an impregnable fort. The walls towered high into the sky. The ground was miles away. No one could survive a fall from those heights. I had heard stories of traitors being dangled over the walls till they begged for mercy and spies being tossed over and then shot as they fell.

The sentries threw me over with a long-practised ease. I fell and fell. I thought of Vishnu and how it might not be bad to be dead after all if it meant being with Vishnu forever, when I found myself landing in a soft place. My eyes, which had been shut tight, opened. A beautiful woman had caught me in her lap, and when she smiled at me, I felt like crying, she reminded me so much of my mother.

The voices I heard from the battlements seemed terribly far

away and unimportant. 'Mother Earth!' the priests were exclaiming. 'Mother Earth herself has received Prahlad into her lap!'

By the time the sentries came racing down to get me, the beautiful woman had vanished and I was wishing she had taken me with her.

The fight, it seemed, wasn't over. Thick ropes were dragged out, each weighed down with rocks. I was tied up, arms bound to my sides, wrapped till I was as helpless as a baby. My mind was far away. I hardly knew what was happening, and frankly, I didn't care. They threw me into the ocean and I sank.

'I know you are with me,' I whispered. 'Vishnu, stay with me.'

I wasn't sinking any more. Instead, the rope snapped, the rocks crumbled and I found myself floating on a wave to the shore. My teacher told me later that for once my father's anger paled in comparison to that of the ocean. After depositing me safely on the soft sand, the ocean had reared up in anger and threatened to drown the earth, to punish Hiranyakashipu for his senseless act of cruelty.

My poor father. He wanted so to be the greatest. Fool that I was, I thought I would try and comfort him.

'It was my friend, Father,' I said. 'I told you he would save me. He is everywhere. Can't you see that?'

My father exploded. I almost expected to see a fire burst out of his head, like it had once before. Instead, he curled his fingers into a fist and struck one of the pillars in the hall where we stood.

'He is, is he? Well then, prove it me! Prove that your god, your friend, is here, right here in this hall, in this pillar. Let me see him, if he is so great! Where is he?'

The pillar shook with the impact of that tremendous fist. The entire court held its breath.

The pillar broke open and a marvellous form appeared. I had never seen anyone like it before but I knew at once who it was. It was Vishnu. His body was a man's and his head a lion's. It was Narasimha, the man-lion. His mane was thick, his eyes were like coals, his mouth was as large as a cave, his tongue was sharper than a newly-whetted sword, and his nostrils breathed fire. His head seemed to touch the sky. The demons dropped their weapons and fled, shrieking. My father stayed where he was.

'This is a new trick by Vishnu!' he roared. 'But I will never be destroyed, for Brahma himself has made me immortal!'

With these words, he rushed at Narasimha. To me, it looked like a moth rushing headlong into a flame. It was courageous and foolhardy. I admired my father and wept for him.

Narasimha had grabbed him, but he wriggled out of his grip. Picking up a mace, he flung it at the man-lion. It bounced off. Everything that was within reach, all the weapons the terrified soldiers had dropped, my father picked up and threw at Narasimha. Spears followed javelins. Elephant hooks followed burning torches. He grew multiple arms and each arm wielded a sword. Finally, he ran towards him with a spear in his hand, too desperate to care. Before

my eyes, I saw Narasimha grab my father and carry him to the palace
gate. I dared not follow for I knew what would happen.

There, at the magical hour of twilight, when it is neither night
nor day, at the threshold of the palace, neither inside nor outside,
neither above the earth or below it, the divine being that was neither
man nor beast, god nor seer, killed Hiranyakashipu with his bare
hands, using neither weapons nor wondrous thunderbolts. Brahma
had kept his promise and yet rid the three worlds of the dreaded
demon-king.

I couldn't stop my tears. My father was dead and I had caused
it, by provoking him to such a murderous rage that he didn't care
if he killed me or died himself. This was not what I had wanted. I
had hoped that by not lifting a finger I could win the battle peacefully
but that was not to be.

The cries of the court and the praises of the gods did little to
make me feel better. They might call me a hero, but what good was
a hero who killed his own father? I howled like a baby, and no one
could understand why.

Suddenly, I felt a soothing presence. I looked up, and I saw Vishnu.
His face was incredibly kind and he said, 'Do not weep my son, it
was meant to be. Your prayers were stronger than Hiranyakashipu's
strongest weapons. You, with the power of your belief alone, brought
me to your side, and achieved what the gods could not. You proved
yourself to be braver than gods or men. Your trials are over, and

because you wish it in the purity of your young heart, your father is forgiven all his evil deeds. Go now, in peace, and weep no more. I will always be with you.'

And he vanished, leaving me quiet and calm. I went back to my studies and in time became the King of the Daityas myself. Some say I make a good king. Some say I am a hero. All I can say is this. A faithful heart can be a more powerful force than anything else. Sometimes that takes a lifetime to find out. Sometimes it happens when you're young. I guess I was just lucky.

The giant's
challenge
echoed
emptily
off the rock face.

t's never easy being the youngest of eight brothers. No one takes you seriously. Everyone, especially your elder brothers, thinks you're a baby, no matter how big you grow, or how smart you become. It's just one of those things. Of course, I'm not saying there aren't any advantages. If your brothers are as cool as mine, they teach you all sorts of useful things. Like how to hide in a tree without making the branches shake. How to whistle like a bird so no one can tell the difference. Or, when you come to think of it, how to make a slingshot that really works, and how to tell whether flat stones or round stones will hit your target better. My brothers taught me all these things and you know what? Before long, I was better than all of them! And though they pretended not to notice, I knew this pleased them no end.

'When we *men* go off to fight, baby brother,' they said to me, rubbing my hair and pulling my cheeks, which I hated and liked at the same time, 'we won't have to worry about who's going to look after Father's sheep. You'll be there won't you, little 'un? Remember, we're counting on you!'

And then they rolled about laughing, as if it was a big joke. But I knew they weren't really joking. And though I objected to them calling me baby brother and calling themselves men, I really couldn't help feeling strangely proud.

Now this war that my brothers were so eager to join had been going on for quite some time. The Israelites, of whom I was one, were fighting the Philistines, of whom I had heard dreadful stories. The leader of our side was called Saul. My brothers were in a state of excitement because the latest news on the war had reached them only a few days ago, and it made them burst with pride as if they themselves had been part of it. My eldest brother Eliab, who is a great storyteller, had explained to me what the fuss was all about.

'Picture this,' he said dramatically, as we all sat in a circle around him. 'Six hundred of our men, camping on the mountainside. They have been fighting since dawn, and many men have fallen. Tired, licking their wounds—no, David, that's just a figure of speech—counting their losses and generally feeling terrible. Saul himself, who otherwise would have gone around the camp, encouraging the men, is lying dispiritedly under a pomegranate tree—yes, David, it could have been a fig tree but that's not really important—too tired to move. You could have cut through the gloom with a knife—no, David, that's yet another figure of speech, and will you stop interrupting me, please?'

That's how Eliab told his stories. And every time, I was the only one who butted in, asking questions about things I didn't understand because how else would I understand them otherwise? Anyway I piped down, and Eliab continued.

'Not exactly an inspiring moment for our army. Some men secretly contemplate running away to the other side. Some slink off and hide themselves in the caves scattered along the face of the mountain. No one wants to think about what lies ahead. Only two people aren't affected by the misery around them—Saul's son Jonathan and his armour-bearer. Huddled in a corner, the two of them whisper to each other.

'"Come on!" says Jonathan, his face shining with suppressed excitement. "Let's cross over to the Philistine camp and see what damage we can do."

'"What if we never come back?" says the armour-bearer, who is not as hot-blooded as his master.

'"Then we never come back!" declares Jonathan stoutly. "Anything is better than sitting around like a bunch of beaten animals! Are you ready? Come!"

'And without waiting for a yes or no from his young companion, Jonathan creeps off to the edge of the camp, taking care not to attract any attention. Not that anyone would have noticed, they are all too busy feeling sorry for themselves. Squeezing past two sharp rocks, they emerge on the Philistine side. A shout goes up.

'"Aha! What have we here! At last the rats come out of their holes! Come, little ratlings, and face us! Or would you rather run back and hide?"

'The Philistine soldiers are heckling the two boys. But what do they care? Running low over the rocks and climbing hand over foot, they meet the first Philistine head on—and kill him! Chance has led them to a good spot. In the narrow gap where they stand, between two sheer faces of rock, not more than one soldier can come up at a time. One by one, the two lads make short work of the Philistines with their flashing swords. The earth shakes, the air vibrates with the clang of metal on metal and the cries of dying men. Consternation in the ranks! Our guards notice the commotion on the other side and run to tell Saul.

'"Count all the men and see who is missing!" Saul orders.

'A quick search follows.

'"Your son Jonathan and his armour-bearer," the answer flies back to him. "Look! See how the Philistines are fleeing!"

'Saul is furious with his son for slipping away into the jaws of death! At the same time, he is delighted with him! Not one to be left behind, he raises a deafening war-cry. The men who were listless rag dolls just a few moments ago charge down the mountainside. It is an avalanche of men! It is like a torrent growing bigger and louder, swelling in volume and strength as the cowards who had hidden themselves in the caves gain heart and join their comrades! It is a glorious sight! The Philistines don't stand a chance! Victory—total and utter—is ours!'

And Eliab wiped his brow, which was glistening with the effort of recreating what must have happened on the battlefield, just as he had told it. I for one believed him, and I know the others did too. No one told stories like Eliab.

. . .

Now I, Samuel, was chosen to be message-bearer, truth-teller and anointer of the king of Israel. When Saul, with the help of his son Jonathan, turned the tide of failure and led his armies into victory, I was told by our Lord to visit Saul in his tent.

'The Lord has sent me to anoint you king of Israel,' I said to him. 'Listen carefully to His words. A great task awaits you—to avenge the wrong done to Israel by Amalek. Go, lead your armies well, and destroy all the Amalekites. When the battle is done, burn everything. Do not keep any of the accursed booty for yourselves. Do you understand?'

Saul nodded his head once, which I took to mean he understood, and then I, Samuel, left.

The news that reached me a few weeks later was both good and bad. Saul had gathered two hundred thousand footmen and ten thousand soldiers of Israel and marched to the city of Amalek. The Amalekites were taken by surprise. The city surrendered and Saul took Agag, the king of Amalek, prisoner and ordered the city to be razed to the ground. This was just as it should have been. But then, folly struck. His soldiers suggested that they take back the fattest sheep and oxen, so that they could make a sacrifice to their god.

And Saul, wise warrior though he was, lost his wisdom and agreed.

That night the Lord came to me and said, 'Saul has disappointed me. He has disobeyed my command. He is not fit to be king. Go and tell him so.'

And so early next morning, I arrived at Saul's tent. He rose to greet me, and said, 'Rejoice! I have destroyed Amalek!'

How could I answer? I could hear the bleating of the lambs they had carried away.

Saul realized what was on my mind and said, 'Those sheep are not for us! Fear not! We only brought them back to honour our Lord with a sacrifice!'

'The Lord does not want sacrifices,' I said. 'All He wants is your obedience. You have failed Him. Now you are no longer fit to be king of Israel!'

Saying this, I left, and Saul retired to his home in Gibeah, filled with sorrow at having failed our Lord.

My sorrow was no less than his. I grieved. I mourned. Seeing this, the Lord took pity on me. He came to me one night and said, 'Listen well, Samuel. Grieve not, for I have chosen a new king. Go and meet Jesse the Bethlehemite. Among his eight sons you will find the new king. You will know him when you see him, and you must anoint him in my name.'

And so I travelled to Bethlehem as ordered. I met Jesse, who was a simple man.

'How will you know who it is?' he asked me, fearfully. That one of his sons should be king of Israel overwhelmed the good man.

'The Lord will guide me,' I answered. 'Now bring me your sons.'

And so Jesse called in his eldest who was named Eliab, then Abinadab, then Shammah. All good strong young lads, fit to be shepherds or soldiers, but not king. Seven of Jesse's sons stood before me, and yet I had not found who I was looking for.

'Have I seen all your children?' I asked Jesse, troubled at heart.

'Yes,' he answered. 'All but my youngest. He is but a child. It cannot be him!'

'Let me see him,' I said. 'For it does not matter how young or old, how tall or short he is. That is what we mortals see. The Lord sees into a person's heart. Bring your youngest in.'

I waited. And then, without warning, a boy burst in, his cheeks rosy like apples, his hair askew, his limbs brown with the sun, and his eyes dancing. I rose to my feet.

'This is the one,' I said. 'Come here, my child, and I will anoint you.'

I, Samuel, had found the new king of Israel.

. . .

I was out on the hillsides as usual when I heard Eliab shouting for me. Later, he told me he shouted for a long time before I answered. You see, I was lying hidden in the grass, flat on my back, chewing a juicy stalk and watching the big white fluffy clouds change shape in the peaceful sky. Right about then, I had spotted an old man with a beard in one of them and I wanted to keep an eye on him in case he gave me the slip as he had done so many times before. It is one of the best things I like about being a shepherd. Once the flock are grazing happily, you can drift about and daydream all you like. No wonder I never heard Eliab till he was almost standing on top of me!

'There you are!' he shouted. 'Stop hiding! Father wants you!'

'Now?' I said, getting up in a hurry. 'But what about the sheep?' I really meant what about my old man in the clouds, but that wouldn't have sounded very responsible, and I wanted Eliab to think well of me. In any case, I couldn't understand why he was looking at me so curiously.

'I'll look after them, silly,' he said, and grabbing me suddenly, gave me a tight hug before pushing me off. 'Go! Run! They are waiting!'

They? Who were they? What was all this fuss about? Not knowing what to expect, I ran all the way home, and burst breathlessly in through the door.

'Father? You sent for me?'

I stopped short. Father was not alone. With him there stood a tall and serious-looking man. He was not from around here. What did he want? Feeling suddenly afraid, I waited, shifting from one foot to another.

'This is the one,' I heard the tall man say in a voice as serious as his face. 'Come here, my child, and I will anoint you.'

What did that mean, anoint? I looked at my father's face, not understanding what the stranger meant. My father had the same curious and proud look I had seen on Eliab's face. Father nodded ever so slightly, which meant that it was all right. The stranger was a friend.

I stepped forward and he blessed me with his large hands and put a sweet-smelling oil on my head and spoke words that I could not understand except that they mentioned the king of Israel, which meant the man had come on the king's duty, and that meant that everything was truly all right.

It didn't take too long. Soon, I was bidding the tall man goodbye and racing out to join my brothers on the hillside. If I had been happy before, I was now in the seventh heaven of happiness, as Eliab would say in one of his fancy figures of speech. Something good had happened to me. It made no difference to things around me, but inside I felt different. Lighter somehow, and wiser. I didn't dare tell my brothers this, of course. They would have laughed till they cried! Their baby brother wiser! What a joke. So I kept this newness to myself and kept larking around as usual.

But new things were in store for me after all. One day, a servant came to our house from the house of Saul and spoke to my father.

'Saul sends me to ask for your youngest son,' the servant said.

'My master is filled with an evil spirit which allows him no sleep, no peace of mind. He needs a person who plays the harp beautifully so that when the music fills his soul, there will be no room for the evil spirit to remain. He has received news that your son David plays the harp like an angel. Send Saul your son, O Jesse, and he will love him as his own.'

I was in the room when he said these words and I must say they made me feel good. No less than Saul, the leader of the Philistines, had heard about me! I wondered what my brothers would have to say about that! I hoped my father would agree to send me off. I needn't have worried. That very day, I set off, a bundle of my things on my back and my little harp in my hand, which I had been taught to play by none other than Eliab himself who played as well as he spoke.

'Don't you disgrace me, baby brother,' he said to me before I left. 'The honour of our family is at stake!'

I didn't disgrace him. That same evening, I played for Saul, who was so moved that he wept. The evil spirit left him and he was well again.

'You truly are an angel, little one,' Saul said to me. 'You have cured an old man. In return, you shall be his armour-bearer.'

Which meant me! I was to be Saul's armour-bearer and bring even greater glory to my family! I could have danced for joy, if I hadn't been surrounded by such grave and serious men! I would march into battle beside Saul, and drive out Philistines just as Jonathan's armour-bearer had done in Eliab's story!

Alas, I had no such luck. Soon after my three eldest brothers joined Saul's army, Saul sent me back to be with my father for a while. The Philistines, it seemed, had regrouped after their series of defeats and were ready for a new fight. Saul was gathering fresh troops and my brothers were among them.

'Your father will be missing his sons,' Saul said to me. 'At least let him have the pleasure of his youngest son's company for a bit!'

And so I was sent home, as if I were still the baby that no one took seriously. Of course, to tell you the truth, I didn't mind that much. Home was a nicer place than Saul's camp, where the beds were rocky and the food scarce.

But after forty days had passed, I began feeling restless. My father noticed this, and calling me to his side, said, 'You have been with me all these days and I have been truly happy. But now it is time for you to return. Take this corn and bread for your brothers, and fight beside them if you must.'

I walked back on the wind, as Eliab would have said. I was so eager to join them and be part of the fight! The camp was easy to see from far. On one side, the Israelites. On the other—the Philistines. All that separated the two armies was a narrow valley. I was not to miss the battle after all! What luck!

Rushing up to my brothers' tent, I greeted them and watched

them eat the corn and bread as if they had been starving for days. All around me was the sound of an army preparing to fight. Mail clanked, swords jangled, steel rang, voices rose and fell. Suddenly a cry of fear cut through the air, like a knife. What was going on? I turned around to face the other mountain and I noticed some movement.

A man had stepped forward from the Philistine camp. Not a man, a giant. While all the other soldiers looked like tiny specks on the mountainside, Goliath looked like a huge chunk of the mountain that had suddenly detached itself, taken human form and begun walking and talking in a voice like thunder.

Goliath!

Who hadn't heard of Goliath! Mothers told naughty children stories about Goliath to make them behave. Grown men fainted at the mention of his name. There wasn't a man among the army that surrounded me who hadn't heard of Goliath, the giant of Gath. Now, there wasn't a man who was not shaking at the mere sight of him.

I examined him closely. This was the stuff of legends, and it was happening before my eyes! It was almost too good to be true. From where I stood he looked more than nine feet and nine inches tall. His head was covered in a massive bronze helmet and his hulking body cloaked in a coat of heavy mail. Thick armour hid his legs, and his breastplate was made of solid bronze. So much metal protecting a man who himself looked as strong as iron! One strike on that armour, and swords and spears would surely snap like sticks! His arms were as heavy and round as clubs, his fists were each the size of a small boulder. One punch from that fist and even the hardiest soldier's jaw would break! And yet, even with fists that were like weapons in themselves, he wielded a tall and deadly spear and held a shield in front of him.

And then he spoke.

'Listen, servants of Saul!' Goliath boomed in our direction. 'Why have you drawn up battle lines if you have no intention of fighting? I am chosen by my people to fight you. Who among you will fight me? Let him show himself. If he kills me in battle, we will be your servants. But if I kill him, then *you* shall be our slaves. Speak!'

The giant's challenge echoed emptily, bouncing off the rock face like hailstones. No one answered. I knew why. Goliath had been known to wipe out entire armies single-handed. Fighting him one-on-one would be sheer suicide. Even Saul would be afraid, and so would every single Israelite.

A deathly hush had replaced the battle-clamour of the camp. I looked around me. No one was looking anyone else in the eye. Hardened battle-scarred faces had turned pasty with fright.

Suddenly, I knew what I had to do.

'I will fight him!' I declared. In that deathly silence, my voice sounded silly. So thin and childish! I wished I had a deeper voice.

Maybe no one had heard me. I was about to say it again when Eliab pounced on me.

'You!' he burst out. 'You're a baby! This isn't a game! You don't understand any of this. Go back to Father at once and stop playing the fool!'

But I was not going to be brushed off so easily. 'I mean it, brother,' I said seriously. 'Take me to Saul.'

Something in my tone must have shown that I meant it. I went to Saul's tent, my three brothers behind me.

'I will fight the Philistine,' I said to Saul. 'No one needs to be afraid, either for me or for himself.'

Saul looked at me strangely. 'It is brave of you, my son, to volunteer,' he said gently. 'But you are a child. Goliath has been a man of war all his life. I cannot let you fight him.'

It was happening again! I was too young, too childish, too weak! I had to assert myself.

'You underestimate me,' I said, in as grown-up a tone as I could manage. 'When I was even younger than I am now, and had just begun tending my father's sheep, a lion and a bear came one night and took away a lamb. I followed them and when they turned on me, claws and teeth bared, I seized first the lion by its mane and killed it, and then the bear. If God saved me from the deadly paws of both the lion and the bear, surely he will not abandon me now.'

Saul was silent for a moment. My brothers looked at me, alarmed at the thought that I was making things up. I looked back at them, boldly, for it was all true.

Then Saul said the words that made my day! 'Well then, go. But not before you're properly armed. Men, attend to the boy at once!'

And Saul's men came up to me with a sword that was too heavy for me and a helmet that was too big and chain mail that was too loose. By the time they were through with me, I couldn't move. It was impossible.

'I cannot wear all this,' I said. 'Take it all off. I'll go just as I am.'

Who was to argue with me now! They took off the helmet and the armour and the mail, and I put down the sword with a sigh of relief and picked up my trusty shepherd's staff. Then I ran to the nearby brook, where I washed my face, which was sweating from all that fussing about, and picked up five smooth pebbles from its bed. I picked them carefully, the way my brothers had taught me, put them into my cloth bag, and sling in hand, I walked towards the Philistine camp.

'At last the Israelites have found a man among them!' the Philistine lookout announced. Everybody stirred. Goliath, who had been resting on the ground, got up, his spear twitching between his lumpy fingers.

'Who is it?' he growled.

I stepped out in front of him.

Goliath laughed. It was like watching the earth quake. His chest heaved as he rasped and howled. 'Not a man! A baby! They snatch a baby from its mother's arms and they push him in front of me. Unarmed, unprotected. Go away, boy, before I die laughing.'

So this Goliath in the end was no different from my brothers, I thought, half angry and half amused. He thought I was a baby. He'd see. My bare feet suddenly felt cold on the stony ground. But I remained where I was.

'I'm not going anywhere,' I said firmly. 'I am here to fight with you, Goliath of Gath.'

'Fight? With what? Your staff? Am I a dog that you would shoo me away with a stick?'

'I am stronger than you think,' I said, the words coming from who knows where. 'You are but armed with a sword and a shield and a spear, while I am armed with faith in my God. My God is the God of the armies of Israel and I will bring you down. Then you will see that God does not save the strong in arms but the strong in faith.'

It was a speech that would have done Eliab proud! How I wished he was there beside me to hear it!

The effect on Goliath was stunning. I could imagine his shock. This audacious little fellow, threatening *him*, Goliath of Gath! For some time he could hardly react. But the army behind him was by now consumed by curiosity and impatient for action. The soldiers all got up and came forward. This flurry of movement brought Goliath back to his senses.

'Stand back, child!' he roared. 'Or else, die!'

I did nothing of the sort. Coolly selecting a stone from my bag, I fitted it into my slingshot and aimed. My aim, as always, was perfect. The stone flew through the air and hit Goliath on the forehead and he crashed face-down to the earth.

The earth shuddered with the impact. Panic spread throughout the Philistine camp. They fled, screaming. It was better than any story Eliab had ever told!

Then, seeing Goliath lying dead, the Israelites poured into the valley and chased the Philistines till not a single one was left to tell the tale of how a boy had killed their strongest warrior, armed with nothing but a slingshot and his faith. How glad I was that boy was me!

THE PARABLE

Will he
**turn me
away**
like a dog?

y brother is a no-good wastrel. He has never done an honest day's work in his life. Father is too kind to him. While the rest of us on the farm are up at the crack of dawn, his highness sleeps on till noon. When the rest of us turn in for a good night's sleep, exhausted by our hard day's work, Mister High-and-Mighty turns up at the nearest tavern in his popinjay finery for a night of unholy carousing. I couldn't be more different from him than chalk from cheese. Nothing gives me more pleasure than the sight of the first green shoots in the field. Not so for my dear brother. For him, pleasure means chasing the pretty girls of the village and bringing a bad name to our house. You'd think he'd outgrow these wild ways, but you'd think wrong. There he sits during harvest time, dreaming idly by the river instead of lending a hand! Really, sometimes I wish I had no brother.

One day, his outrageous behaviour reaches the limit. He goes up to my father, as jaunty as a jaybird, and says, in that annoyingly cheerful voice of his, 'Father! I have a brilliant idea! Instead of waiting for my share of your property, why don't I take it now? That way, I don't have to spend the rest of my life on this mouldy old farm, and you don't have to break your head trying to make me stay. Give me my share and let me be off. Less headaches all around!'

Mouldy old farm indeed! If I were my father, I would have thrashed him. But like I said, my father is too kind. He takes out a pen and parchment, as soft as you please, and draws up a new arrangement. The wastrel comes out looking for me, and whistling between his teeth, says, 'Bye bye brother! I'm off to see the world!'

For a moment I think my father has finally cut him off without a penny, as he rightly should. I go in, and what do you know? My father tells me half his property is now the young scallywag's! I have no say, it seems, no voice as the elder brother. Ah well. It is Father's property, he does with it what he wishes.

One good thing came of all this though. The farm was soon to be rid of the pest. When it came to selling his part of Father's estates, my brother showed himself to be very efficient! Oh yes, one day he was showing buyers around, next day he was counting gold coins into a thick old pouch. Mister Smarty-Pants himself! He left immediately, his clothes in the stout wooden box that had lain in the attic, and his hat rakishly on his head. Not a word of farewell, mind you. I didn't expect any. But Father did. I could tell at breakfast he was grieving. What did my dear brother care! He was off to see the world. And if you asked me—good riddance to bad rubbish too!

. . .

I couldn't stop singing! Or—when I ran out of words—whistling. It felt so good to have the farm behind me and the open road before me. My glowering elder brother would now have no one to glower at, and Father would have no complaints. Not that he did anyway. That is one thing I must say about the old man. He's always been very decent to me, no matter what everyone said. Very decent of him in fact to let me go. Catch any other father parting with his wealth in his own lifetime! No siree. So here I am, walking as if on air, singing.

Everything I see tells me I was right to leave. I always knew our village was dull. But now when I see these towns and cities, I realize just how dull! In the cities, the taverns are open all night, the women are far prettier and far easier to get along with, and the men are altogether more dashing. I myself had to get a completely new wardrobe to keep myself from being stared at for my country bumpkin ways. And back home, they thought I was a rake! It makes me laugh.

I have a lot to learn. Conversation for example. In the cities everyone makes sparkling conversation. Not the occasional grunt my brother passes off as speech! Poor fellow, if only he learned to have a bit of fun! As for me, I picked up city ways very fast. And made friends even faster. I found myself a boarding house and soon was quite a hit in town! It's funny how much people like me. There I'll be sitting with a pitcher of wine, and a stranger comes up, slaps me on the back and starts up a conversation. Naturally, I ask him to join me, and soon we have a party going. Jolly lads, all of them! The least I can do in return for being made to feel so at home is buy them all a round of drinks, and then another, and another. Time passes so fast in these places, you hardly realize when it's sun-up and time to totter home, singing a last gay song! I tell you, this is the life!

Of course, it isn't all fun and games. We do serious business too. We keep an eye out for our creditors, and make ourselves mysteriously unavailable when they arrive. We pool in all our money and figure out the most enjoyable ways of spending it. And, of course, if one of our gang is really hard up, we kind souls bail him out. In fact, I find myself bailing out a lot of these poor lads who have no head for figures like I do. It pleases me to be of some use. Of course, they all love me for it. True, my pouch is a lot lighter these days, but who cares? What is money for if not to spread a little cheer?

I must have miscalculated.

One morning, or rather mid-morning, for I had slept only at dawn, I was woken by a godawful racket. Someone was trying to break down my door!

'Stop it!' I said, or rather, mumbled.

No effect. I would have to force open my eyes and clear those vocal cords.

'Go away!' I managed to shout.

'I will, young sir,' said my landlord's voice, deceptively sweet. 'But only after you pay last month's rent. And the month before. Give me the money, and I'm gone!'

'Oh, go away!' I said, really annoyed by now. 'You old fool!'

The door crashed open. The landlord, whom I had so rashly called an old fool, stood there, not a trace of sweetness on his face.

'Up, young man,' he said. 'If you haven't got the money, as I suspect you haven't, it'll be *you* that's leaving, not me!'

It was useless to argue. I turned out my pockets half-heartedly, knowing I would find nothing. The landlord literally booted me out and insisted on keeping the stout wooden trunk with the brass clasps that Father had treasured all these years. But what could I do? I wasn't going to stay behind and sweep rooms to pay off my debt. No siree! I was off, to find shelter with some kind friend, no doubt.

No doubt I had miscalculated again. Not a single lad in what I so fondly called 'our gang' would have me. No place old chum, wife's family is visiting, old mum's ill, leaving town myself—all sorts of excuses came pouring in, but not a single offer of help. All the jolly lads and pretty dames pretended they didn't even know me! All the poor lads I had helped out looked embarrassed but did nothing. I was deeply hurt. I decided to leave town.

And just then, as if fate herself was my enemy, a great famine struck. Everywhere you went people were dying like flies. I was just one among many hungry and miserable souls, homeless and penniless. Who would spare a thought for me?

Hunger drove me to make a desperate decision. I, who had never done a stroke of work in my life, as my elder brother was so fond of pointing out, decided to look for work. It galled me, it stung my pride, but hunger pangs stung me even more. I knocked on many doors. Can you hoe, can you till, can you sow, they kept asking me and I kept saying no, no, no. What would you sow or hoe or till anyway, the countryside was ravaged, but still they asked, for I was passing through farm country and only a farm boy would do. At last, I came to a farm where the man cast a disgusted look at my by-then ragged and disreputable appearance and barked, 'What are you good at then?'

'Nothing much, sir,' I said, and bit my tongue. 'I mean, anything. I can do anything, sir!'

'Hmmm,' the man said. 'In that case, let me see how good you are at feeding swine!'

Swine! My heart rebelled. A landowner's son, a rich man once, to tend swine. I squashed my revulsion and took the job. Every morning I took the pigs their feed and watched them as they fed greedily on the scraps and leftovers they were given. It was a disgusting sight. They grunted and grubbed about in the trash and snorted and gobbled. It made me sick. And yet I couldn't take my eyes away. Day after day I did this. The food my employer gave me was hardly better than what he gave his pigs. In fact, worse, for the quantities were far less. As I watched, I felt a desperate craving to throw myself into the pig's trough and bury my face in their food. Just one scrap for the yawning pit that was my stomach! Just one . . . I leaned forward, I bent. I almost fell in . . .

I came to my senses.

What am I doing here, I asked myself angrily. This man treats his pigs better than his workers. On Father's farm, every worker had not just enough food for himself, but lots more to take home to his family! And here I am starving to death, grubbing with the pigs! What a fool I was to leave. Fool, fool, fool! But how can I go back? What can I say? Father, forgive me? Will he? Or will he turn me away like a dog? I have to try. 'Don't accept me as your son, but let me be one of your hired men,' I'll say to him. Surely he will, he is kind, he always has been. Get up! Leave!

I got up and left. It was as easy as that. How different the trudge back home was! I was weary and dispirited. I was nervous. I was entering familiar territory. Here is where I sat, laughing at the workers for being so industrious. Here is where I spent whole nights, carousing. Here is where my property once stood, that I sold. And here is my father's land!

I had arrived. The sight stabbed me through the heart. Famine had not touched these parts. The fields shone golden with corn. The air smelt sweet. I stumbled on. There, my father's house, the same but not the same. Some parts were newer, bigger. They had been rebuilding, repainting the old farm! Maybe my brother was getting married! Maybe I would interrupt a cosy family scene. Maybe I should not proceed any further. But my feet wouldn't listen and I kept staggering on, too tired to even think. Surely they would slam the door in my face? Surely they wouldn't accept me.

Surely . . . that wasn't my father running towards me, his head uncovered, his arms outstretched?

It was him. He was running towards me and he was crying. I couldn't walk any more. I fainted.

. . .

It had been a good day on the farm. The corn was thriving. It would be a good harvest. The best in years, in fact. After that no-good wastrel left, it seems our fortunes have only got better. He took his bad star with him, wherever he went. I urged my horse on a little faster. A good supper, and then a quiet evening by the fire before bed. This was the life!

I crested the hill and stopped short.

All the lights in the house were blazing. The windows were all open and the sound of music and dancing came streaming out into the evening air. Voices shrieked with laughter and hands clapped and feet stomped. What was going on in my house?

I galloped down.

'What is going on?' I asked the stable boy who had rushed up to take my horse. 'Do we have unexpected guests?'

'Yes indeed, young master, and the most unexpected of them all!' said the stable boy, who was always too talkative for my liking. 'It's your brother, young master! He has returned and the old master has ordered the fatted calf to be killed for tonight's feast! And he said to me, "Hurry, bring me my finest robe that my younger son may wear it, **and** fetch my softest sandals for his poor aching feet, and bring me my ring that I may slip it on his finger!" And then the little master woke up for he had fainted and they embraced each other and cried! It was a grand sight, young master, and Cook says she has never seen a happier day!'

What? The wastrel returned? Impossible. And the fatted calf slaughtered for him, who had walked away with half our father's wealth and undoubtedly squandered it on unmentionable pleasures? Impossible. But there it was—the house brimming with gaiety and the servants rushing to and fro with platters.

It was unthinkable.

I clenched my fists, so dearly would I have liked to knock that blackguard down!

'What are you waiting for?' my father's voice came floating out, cheerily. 'Come in and see who's home!'

Something inside me snapped. Such joy in the old man's voice I had not heard ever since my brother left.

'No, I won't,' I said. 'Not if that scoundrel is in there. Besides, you don't need me. You are merry enough, I can see.'

My father said nothing. A second later, I realized he was standing beside me.

'Do not be angry my son,' he said, gently. 'Come in and embrace your brother. He is a changed man. You will see for yourself. Do not spoil the wonderful thing that has happened today. Your brother is home, safe and sound, and a better man too!'

I exploded.

'A better man!' I said, bitterly. 'And what am I then, Father, who have been by your side all these years, slaving on your fields, never going against anything you say, serving you all my life? In all these years, never once have you said, "Son, call your friends and celebrate." Not once have you given me even a young goat that I may throw a feast and rejoice! And when he comes home, the son who threw away your fortune on taverns and women, for that scoundrel you kill the fatted calf, and throw a feast fit for kings!'

He came closer to me and he held me. My shoulders were shaking. I was ashamed for I was crying with fury and with grief, but still he held me.

'My son!' he said. 'You mistake me. Your place in my heart is assured. You have always been with me and everything I own is yours. No one can ever take your place! But your younger brother— him I had lost to the wicked ways of the world. He was dead all these years, and only now has he really begun to live! Don't you see why I must celebrate? All these years, I had a younger son, and you a younger brother, only in name. Today we both have him in truth, at last! Come, grieve no longer and let us feast by his side.'

I felt calm. All my anger seemed to have flowed out with my

tears. My father had comforted me in a way that made me feel more loved than I have been all my life. I took the hand he gave me and together we went into the house. I embraced my brother and our feast of thanksgiving continued late into the night.

The only thing
I wanted,
I didn't have.

y only son ran away from home. It is hard to describe the heartache that follows when you lose your only son. Ours was a poor family, so poor we would often have only one crust of bread between the two of us. Sometimes, not even that. My boy would sleep hungry and I would lie awake, trying to think of a way to improve my situation. But it was difficult. His mother had died when the boy was very young. I had tried to be both mother and father to him, but I had failed. And so, one day, he ran away.

I went crazy, looking for him. There was nothing to hold me in my hometown anyway. The morning I discovered his bed empty and his pitiful belongings gone, I left too. I had no idea where I was going. All I knew was that if I didn't look for him, I would lose my mind.

Every passer-by I met, I stopped and asked, 'Have you seen a little boy, about that high, hair all mussed up, with a little bundle of clothes on his shoulder?' I knew it was useless even before I asked, but still I asked. They shook their heads, gave me advice, pointed out quite the wrong boys and in general added to my complete despair. I lost track of how many towns and villages I travelled through, or how much distance I put between me and my past.

Sometimes an awful thought occurred to me. What if my boy had returned to our home, and found it empty? What then? Where would he look for me? How would he ever find me? Would he think I had abandoned him, like a stray dog? The thought hurt me so much, I sometimes cried out loud. Most often, however, I tried to quell it completely. He would not go back there. I *would* find him.

I didn't. One day, I knew I could go no further. He was lost, my boy. I could wander the whole earth but still I would not find him. My pain had now become a part of me. Like a foot or a hand, I carried it everywhere. I decided to stop searching and settle down in the town I found myself. Any town was like any other, as far as I was concerned. All empty and sad.

I settled down and started my own trade. My heart was not in it, but as if to spite my melancholy, everything I touched prospered. Soon I had a series of warehouses, overflowing with grain. My coffers filled up with gold and silver, crystal and coral. My farms (oh yes, farms!) soon became known for having the woolliest sheep and the finest cows, the plumpest goats and the swiftest horses. My wagons were the rage in every town, so luxurious and dandy were they! I, who had once lived on a crust of dry bread, had a retinue of servants to look after my every need. There wasn't a single rich or powerful man in the region who didn't come calling on me.

And still my heart ached. When people envied me openly, I pitied them. What did they know of what lay in my heart? What was the use of all this wealth when my life was a wasteland, bereft of son and heir, fear and anxiety my only companions? I could see my so-called friends biding their time, waiting for the moment when I would die and they would lay their greedy hands on my fortune. I had everything in the world. But the one thing I wanted, I didn't have. My son.

It happened on one of the days when I received local nobility. I was, as usual, bored. There I sat, on a lion-couch gifted to me by a prince, my feet resting on a jewelled footstool. To my right and left sat priests and warriors, merchants and noblemen. Behind each chair stood an attendant. I had only to snap my fingers to have goblets of wine and trays of food brought out. Someone was making a long and flattering speech, at the end of which I knew would come a request for something or another. I would have respected them more if they came straight out with it. At least I would be saved this tedium. Trying to stifle a yawn, I pressed my lips tightly and looked away, as if reflecting deeply on what the speaker was saying.

That's when I saw him. My son.

He stood at my gate, a man now, thin and scruffy. He looked hesitant and lost. He looked nothing like the boy I remembered, but I knew without a doubt, it was him. The impossible surge of joy that filled my whole being told me I was right.

I almost leapt out of my seat and ran to the gate. But something held me back.

'Quick!' I said, interrupting what the flattering merchant was saying, not taking my eyes off my son. 'Bring that man to me! Hurry, he's leaving!'

And so he was! With my heart in my mouth I watched the thin man turn abruptly away, his head bent down, his legs scampering, as if afraid of being noticed. My guards wasted no time. In seconds, they were after him. By this time, he had started running. 'O don't let him go,' I prayed, oblivious of the flutter my odd behaviour was causing among my guests. I could not bear the thought of losing my son all over again. But it seemed like I would.

Ah—the guards had caught him, but he seemed reluctant to come. 'Why are you arresting me,' I could hear a piteous voice saying. 'I was only standing and looking, I promise. Please, let me go!' He struggled and shuddered in their grip like a trapped animal. And the more he struggled the more the guards tightened their grip. Suddenly, he went slack. My son had fainted, from fright or hunger or both, I could not tell.

I couldn't bear this torture any more.

'Stop!' I called, getting up from my chair so they would hear me. 'Do not bring him to me by force. Sprinkle some cold water on his face and when he revives, let him go.'

My heart broke, just saying those words. After all these years, to see the son I had given up for dead, and then pretend I did not know him! It was too much. But still, it had to be done. My son was in too feeble a state to believe that this grand person with the mansion and million servants was his own father! He would think it was a heartless joke, and run away again at the first opportunity. I could not let that happen. No, I could not thrust myself back into my son's life so suddenly. I would have to think of a better way.

And so, with breaking heart and straining eyes, I watched the young man who was my son get up slowly, and then, quite bewildered by the guards' change of attitude, walk away from me, not looking back even once.

I dismissed the gathering. There were murmurings and mutterings, but I couldn't be bothered. I had a son to reclaim. I called two of my most trusty servants and told them to follow the poor young man who had fled so suddenly. 'See where he goes, get talking to him and offer him work,' I said to them. I had a feeling being offered work by two shabby but decent hardworking men would be easier for my son to take.

Waiting was agony. What if I had been wrong? What if my son had already become untraceable, just as he had all those years ago? 'If he accepts,' I had told my men, 'take him to the workers' huts, and make him feel at home. Let me know only later.'

Next morning brought good news. My son had agreed at once, they said. 'We are scavengers,' they had told him, 'and we need an extra pair of hands.' That night, he had eaten a bowl of soup as if he hadn't seen food for a long time and told them how he got to be so desperate. His father was very poor, the two men told me, not realizing how every word made me cringe. He couldn't stand that sort of life so he ran away, thinking things would be better elsewhere.

314

It didn't turn out as he had imagined. Out on the roads, he had to beg for his food, and very soon his clothes were torn and his shoes worn out. He slept under hedges or in abandoned barns. He was chased out of fields by barking dogs or angry farmers. In cities, he was invariably mistaken for a pickpocket and given a thrashing simply for hanging around, looking hopefully at the rich men who passed. He soon came to have a horror for rich men, he said, for they all seemed to be terribly fierce and cruel. He did odd jobs for a few coins that disappeared before he knew it. As he grew older, it became harder for him to get by, for while a kind woman might offer a bowl of soup to a hungry young boy, she would think twice about inviting a strange young man into her house.

So that had been his life all these years! I marvelled at the strange twist of fate that had brought him to the very town where I had settled. His horror of richness was just as extreme as his horror of poverty had once been. Poor boy! I would have to be patient with him.

It was hard, but I managed. I got news of him being a conscientious worker. One day, when they were working in the fields closest to the house, I saw with a jolt how haggard and pinched my son looked. His clothes were smeared with dust, his hands and face were filthy. Unable to bear the pretence any more, I decided to meet him. Not the way I was—that would merely send him into a panic again. No, I took off my rich robes and my jewels, smeared my face with dirt, and picking up a workbasket, made my way towards the labourers.

'Get on with your work,' I called out to the men, as if I were their overseer. 'Don't laze around!'

When I reached my son, I paused. My hands were shaking. I steadied myself and said, 'You are a good worker, my son. I have never seen you grumbling or getting into fights or going off for a nap under the bushes. It is rare to get a worker like you. The master is very happy with you and has told me that I am to increase your wages. Not just that, you are to have everything you wish—more rice, wheat, salt, vinegar—anything you need, just ask and it will be provided.'

The smile that appeared on my poor son's face was like a balm to my sore spirit! I arranged it just as I said. My son continued to live in his little hut, but I made sure it was now very comfortable with a soft bed to sleep in, fine dishes to eat out of and food that came directly from my kitchen. As if to prove worthy of this special attention, my son worked even harder, which made it easy for me to put him in charge of the other workers. Seeing his self-respect coming back, I asked him to come to the house and meet the 'master'. No more disguises.

He was a changed man! I could see by the confident way he walked in, and the care with which he was dressed, that he was no longer frightened by the pomp and glory of a rich man's establishment. I knew exactly how he felt. He was no longer a desperate fugitive, hiding and hounded, perpetually hungry, perpetually at someone's mercy. He was a man trusted by the master and respected by the workers. He took pride in being invaluable. He probably laughed at how scared he had been on that first day he saw me!

My plan was working well. We grew closer. Though he maintained a certain distance, it was clear that the affection between us was growing. How often I longed to break the barrier and clasp him to my heart! But still I waited. The moment had to be just right.

Some time later, I fell ill. I didn't dare wait any longer. Calling my son into my bedchamber, I said, 'Listen, my son (for that is what I always called him, which my son considered a mere gesture of affection), I have not much longer to live. No, do not weep, it is true, and we must face it. I want you to understand fully the workings of my estate. You must take stock of all that is there in my granaries and treasuries. Once you have done that, I will tell you how they are to be distributed and used once I am gone. There is no one I trust as much as you.'

He left the room struggling to control his tears. When he told me he was ready, I invited all the leading citizens of the town, the priests, the warriors, the merchants and all the neighbouring kings and nobles. They arrived. I made my son stand beside me. And then I addressed the gathering.

'Thank you for coming so quickly,' I said to the grand assembly. 'I have called you here today for a special reason. As you all know, I am ailing, and any day now may be my last. Before I go, I would like you all to know who is to inherit my estate.'

A buzz filled the room. An heir! The childless master was about to announce an heir! Young grandees and dashing young noblemen who had spent hours flattering me stirred expectantly in their seats. Everyone looked at everyone else. Only my son looked stricken, the thought of my dying grieved him so.

'The man you see standing by my side,' I continued. 'I have loved him like a son. All of you know how important he has been to me. But what you do not know is that this man is not just my son in name, he is my real son, my one and only child.'

I could feel my son stiffen. What was the master saying? I went on.

'Many years ago, my son ran away from home. We were poor then and maybe I was not a good father. I went after him, I searched high and low, but in vain. I settled in a strange land, took a new name and prospered. But it was all meaningless without my son. Then one day he arrived, unknowing, at my doorstep and failed to recognize his old father. He was terrified of everything I had become, and I would have lost him all over again, if I had not found another way of keeping him by my side. And so I made him, gradually, my

318

trusted aide, and now he is ready to be called my son by all who are here today!'

The audience burst into cheers. (I could tell the disappointed grandees were looking daggers at my son, the man they had thought was a menial!) My heart beat wildly. I turned to look at my boy. The tears were streaming down his cheeks. He knelt in front of me and wept unabashedly, there in front of the whole company. I stroked his head. I could hardly speak, I was so choked with emotion.

'My son, my son! How I have waited for this moment, when you would be ready to accept me as your own! You are my heir and all I have is yours! Rise and never leave me again for as long as I live.'

And he never did.

THE GODLY
ANIMAL

What
dragged so
horribly
and slowed him
down?

We had marched to the very edge of the land. In front of us lay the sea, heaving and billowing. The waves were flecked with foam, and in galloping ranks they raced towards the shore and broke in a crash of white noise. We, who had travelled so far, through so many lands, had never seen anything like it. It was just water, liquid and shapeless, but it robbed our mighty army of all its might. We stood there and stared.

'At least a hundred leagues to Lanka!' said Angad, the chief, shading his eyes as he peered out to the island that seemed to bob among the waves, like a boat. 'A full hundred leagues to the island where she may be!'

The monkey host groaned. You cannot imagine the size of that groan. Imagine instead the size of the monkey host. File upon file of warriors, gathered from all corners of the world. They came from north and south, from east and west, raising mighty columns of dust as they marched. They left their homes and their families and came in answer to the call of Sugriva, the monkey king. Some were golden, the sun's bright sheen trapped in their silky fur. Some were silver, shafts of moonlight rippling as they walked. Some were green as lotus stems and some were as white as untrodden Himalayan snow. It was a mesmerising sight, that host of valiant fighters! They gathered in tens of thousands before Sugriva, and Sugriva spoke.

'Welcome, my legions!' he said. 'It thrills this old king's bones to see you here, so young and brave! Listen then, to your task. I

324

would not be standing here, your king once again, if it were not for two men. You see them beside me. Their names are Rama and Lakshman and they are the exiled sons of Dasaratha. With their help I have killed Bali, who had wrested my throne. In return, I promised them my help. In truth, I promised and I forgot and would have been unworthy of my word if Hanuman had not reminded me what I owed. And so, roused from my revelry, I summoned you, my legions!'

The legions cheered.

'We are to help find Rama's gentle wife,' Sugriva continued. 'Sita is her name, and she has been cruelly abducted by the demon-king Ravan. No one knows where he has taken her. We have news, leads, but much time has passed and the trail grows cold. You, my legions, must search for her. Search everywhere, in every forest, mountain and plain. No cave nor cranny, no grove nor gorge should go unturned. March, and do not return till you have found her!'

With a cry that rocked the sky, the monkey host began their search. I, Jambavan, King of the Bears, went with them, and so did Hanuman, devoted chieftain, and Angad, Bali's good son. And how we searched! At first, we were directionless. Then the dying Jatayu brought us news that quickened our steps and veered our course. 'Lanka,' he said. 'Ravan has taken her to Lanka!'

Nothing had stopped us, not the highest mountain or the thickest jungle. Until now. A hundred leagues, three hundred miles of uncrossable sea lay between Lanka and us. The island, so tantalizingly within sight and so infuriatingly out of reach . . .

And so, the monkey host groaned. A colossal, collective sigh of despair. To be so close and yet so far!

Angad, good prince that he was, may have felt the same, but he did not show it. Instead, he addressed the monkey host, hoping, I know, against hope. 'Do not let despair numb you!' he cried. 'We have a promise to keep and a king to obey. Who among you will make the leap to Lanka and bring glory to the tribe?'

One by one, the chiefs came forward. 'Seventy miles is my farthest leap,' said Gaja. 'One hundred and forty,' said Gavaksha.

'Two hundred and ten,' said Gavaya.

Till finally, good Angad said, 'I might make the leap of three hundred miles across, but no way will I be able to leap back!'

It was time for me to speak.

'Listen, good Angad,' I said. 'Even if you could, it is not right that you should go. You are the leader of this host, you must stay alive and lead it, not perish! Once upon a time *I* could have leapt a hundred leagues, three hundred miles and more! But now I am old, my hair is grey and my fire dimmed. But listen, I know of a chief among you mighty enough for this task!'

Excitement surged through the monkey host. I hushed them with my grizzled paw.

'He does not know it, but he is rich in power, strength and skill. He is learned and indestructible, ardent and wise. He stands among you now, downcast and oppressed, forgetting all that he is and can be. He is Hanuman!'

As one, the monkey host turned to look at him. There he stood, nonplussed. I continued.

'Hanuman is more than Sugriva's wise counsellor and fearless chief, more than Rama's devoted friend and more than Angad's champion fighter. He is the Wind God Vayu's son!'

Another surge of excitement convulsed the crowd.

'His mother was Anjana, a beautiful apsara who came to live on earth as a monkey. One morning, as the sun rose over the crown of a hill, Hanuman thought it was a fruit hanging from one of the trees on the hill. Filled with childish glee, he leapt three hundred leagues into the air towards it and swallowed it whole. The Sun God blazed red-hot in his throat with anger, but little Hanuman didn't care! Indra saw what had happened. He had to do something to rescue the ball of fire on which life depended. So he raised his red-hot bolt and aimed it at little Hanuman. Hanuman fell out of the sky on to a rock. His jaw broke, and the Sun God came out, safe.

'But Vayu was not pleased! Seeing his son lying bleeding on the ground, he got so angry that he commanded all the breezes to stop blowing. The north wind, the south wind, the east wind and the west wind, they all stopped. The air stood absolutely still. Not a leaf rustled. Animals suffocated. Human beings choked. No living thing could survive that dead calm. So all the gods got together and went to Vayu. "Make the winds blow again," they said, "and we will each grant your son a boon that will make him stronger and wiser than any other creature on earth."

'Vayu agreed and Hanuman became the mightiest creature of all. But he was too young for such powers! To him, his powers were only good for pranks! He summoned up violent winds when sages were meditating and then sprang away, laughing. So uncontrollable did he become, that the sages cursed him. "Till someone reminds you, O Hanuman," they said, "you will forget your powers and be as any other monkey chief, strong of arm and broad of chest, but no more!"'

The host exclaimed. Hanuman's princely face was suddenly flushed with recollection. As we watched, he grew in size. Bigger and bigger, till he was as tall as the sea was wide.

'Your arms are as mighty as Garuda's wings!' I said. 'Vayu himself has given you a stride to match his own. Our lives depend on you. Rise and do what you must!'

With a leap, Hanuman wheeled into the sky and landed on the peak of the mountain Mahendra. The great mountain swayed, the trees shook, the birds and animals fled. The grass glinted like green gems as Hanuman went striding across. Pink, blue, white and red lilies bloomed wherever he stepped. The light was alive with rainbow colours and the lakes rippled. Hanuman prayed to the Sun and the Wind Gods and to Indra, and then spoke to us from the crest of the mountain.

'Like a shaft shot from Rama's bow I will fly to Ravan's island, and if I do not find Sita there, I will fly into the heavens looking for her, and if I fail to find her even then, I will bring you Ravan himself!'

He sprang from the mountain top across the vast sea gulf, and the power of his leap shook the waters till they gushed and foamed and the breeze caused by his passing stirred up a tempest. The magic hill of Mainaka burst out of the ocean to give the monkey chief a place to rest and catch his breath, but Hanuman cried out, 'I must not stop! Now is not the time to ease my weary limbs! But I thank you, noble hill!' And he continued his great leap, till he was a speck in that deep blue sky.

Our wait was long. Nothing is as fretful as an idle army! We scanned the horizon every minute for Hanuman's return. The sea had turned glassy, reflecting the sky in its still surface. It was as if the sea was waiting too.

Suddenly we saw thick whorls of cloud spiralling into the sky where the island of Lanka stood.

'Lanka burns,' Angad said worriedly. 'I hope no harm has come to Hanuman!'

I shook my head. 'No one can harm Hanuman,' I said, but still my old heart ached from not knowing for certain.

The clouds were red-rimmed and smoke-grey. They shifted and shook in the sky, as we did on the shore. Suddenly the monkey host gave a cheer. 'He returns!' they shouted and rushed to climb the hill on which he had landed. 'Tell us,' they shouted, 'tell us everything!'

And Hanuman, without pausing for breath, told his story.

It had not been an easy crossing. As he flew, like a mountain with wings, a rakshasa sprang out of the sea. Her teeth were mean and her breath scorching. She opened her mouth wide, and to escape being swallowed whole, Hanuman grew ten leagues in height. But in return, the demon's mouth grew twenty leagues. The bigger Hanuman grew, the bigger her mouth became. At last, in a flash of inspiration, Hanuman suddenly made himself very tiny, slipped in and out of her mouth and bounded out of reach.

The rakshasa howled to find she had been outwitted. A second demon heard her and spotted the great monkey coming. 'Today at last my hunger will be met!' she thought, drooling and slobbering. As Hanuman passed over her, casting a great shadow on the water, she seized the shadow and tried to pull him down like the wind tugging at a ship's sail. He felt a dead weight on his arms and legs.

He could see nothing near him. What dragged so horribly and slowed him down? At last, he spotted the demon and rushed to fight her. As she opened her jaws and swallowed him, he grew bigger in size till she was torn into two. Hanuman burst out unharmed, leaving the demon lying dead in the water.

The praises of the gods and spirits of the air ringing in his ears, he saw the thickly-wooded green shore of the island of Lanka before him, and with one final burst of energy, landed on the peak of a mountain. He was in the land of Ravan, at last. He had made the crossing no one else could have.

Changing guise at will, he found his way to the grove where Sita was kept, guarded by a band of she-demons. Making himself tiny, he hid in the trees, waiting for a chance to reveal himself as Rama's messenger. Finally, when he heard the sound of the guards snoring at the other side of the grove, he spoke to her. He praised the mighty king Dasaratha's moon-bright son Rama, the warrior who gave up everything in order to obey his father and who wandered through the wilds with Sita, his wife and Lakshman, his brother, only to lose Sita to the demon-king Ravan. He sang eulogies to the courage of the grieving husband who saved the monkey kingdom in return for the monkey king's help to find and rescue her, his wife.

Hearing this disembodied voice coming from a tree, Sita was alarmed. Was this some kind of trick? But just then, Hanuman appeared before her and bowed deeply. His courteous behaviour, his well-chosen words and the sight of her husband's ring calmed Sita and filled her with hope.

'Do not fear, gentle lady!' Hanuman said. 'We will be back to save you. I must now return to your lord.'

And he was about to leap off again, when the guards awoke and descended on him with cries of rage. He destroyed them all. Ravan's son Indrajit came riding out on a chariot drawn by four tigers. Hanuman leapt up to dodge Indrajit's arrow, but the demons cast a spell on him and he was struck down. He fell from the sky and the demon-soldiers tied him up as he lay stiff and unable to move, and carried him jubilantly to their king.

Hanuman, tied up as he was, said to the demon-king, 'Before you kill me, listen carefully, Ravan! It is not too late to repent even now! Do so and you will be forgiven. Persist and ruin will fall upon you, your family, your subjects and your kingdom.'

But Ravan was not about to listen to a monkey, however fierce and powerful he might look. He said, 'You are right. I cannot kill you, for that would be discourteous, but I can punish you for daring to show your face here. You shall go back to your master, but in disgrace. Guards! Set his tail afire!'

The guards soaked strips of cloth in oil and wrapped them around Hanuman's tail. Then, with whoops of mirth, they set fire to the cloth and watched it sizzle. With much beating of drums and blowing of horns they paraded him through the streets, shouting, 'Here goes the human-king's monkey-spy!'

The fire burned into Hanuman's fur and flesh. The pain was excruciating, but he bore it without a whimper. Suddenly, though his tail was still a torch of fire, he felt no pain. 'It must have been Sita, who prayed to Agni, the God of Fire, to save me,' Hanuman said. 'She prayed and I felt no pain.'

Determined to leave his mark on Lanka, Hanuman jumped on to the roofs and set first one, then another house on fire with his blazing tail. Palaces, mansions, citadels, towers, courtyards, squares— soon the whole of Lanka was a raging bonfire. Vayu fanned the flames, and the sky was shot through with clouds of smoke.

It was time to return. Hanuman made himself small and the bonds came loose and fell away in a heap. With one last look at the burning city, he leapt into the sky and landed amidst us.

Hanuman had fulfilled his mission!

News went to Sugriva and before long he joined us along with Rama and Lakshman. Under the watchful eye of Nala, one of Sugriva's ablest chiefs, the monkey host built a massive bridge out of trees and stones. It was an unshakeable bridge. Thousands and thousands of feet tramped across without causing even a tremor. The air shook but not the bridge. The army stormed Ravan's city and the battle began.

It was a merciless battle. The demons used every trick they could.

Spells, magic, missiles—nothing was spared. On both sides, great heroes fell one by one. Finally, Ravan himself came to the battlefield. He was determined to wipe out Vibhishan, his brother, who had become Rama's friend and ally. Fang-toothed spears and ferocious javelins, wicked spikes and brutal maces flew fast and furious. The air bristled with arrows. Vibhishan killed Ravan's horses with his club. With a roar, Ravan hurled his spear at Vibhishan but Rama's arrows stopped it. Ravan picked up an even mightier spear and this time Vibhishan would have breathed his last if Lakshman hadn't struck the demon-king with *his* arrows and diverted Ravan's wrath to himself.

'Since my brother's life is so dear to you, allow me to take yours instead!' Ravan shouted and flung the deadly spear at Lakshman. Lethal and unerring, the spear struck Lakshman and he fell.

Rama was disconsolate. 'I cannot go on without you, Lakshman!' he said, tears running down his face as he cradled his brother in his arms. 'All my courage deserts me. How can I fight when my dearest brother is dead?'

Grief-stricken, Hanuman watched his lord. Seeing Lakshman's pale and rigid face and Rama's unstoppable tears, he felt an awful pain. It was as if he himself had fallen, the pain was so sharp.

But then the physician spoke. 'Do not lose heart, Rama! Your brother is not dead yet. Look at his brow, it still has the faintest glow of life. His skin is clear and his palms are still as pink as fresh lotuses. If I can get him a certain herb before sunrise, he will live.'

'Where is this herb?' Rama said, his voice dull with grief.

'On the peak of the Mahodaya grows the Sanjivani herb. I must have it before dawn.'

'Alas! Then he will die, for no one can find it so soon,' said one of the monkey chiefs.

'He will *not* die!' said Hanuman, stepping forward. 'I will go and fetch it!' And with one leap, he was gone.

This wait seemed longer. We scanned the horizon again, but this time fearfully, dreading the first glimpse of dawn. I myself had been wounded. I lay on the battlefield, countless shafts in my side, weaker than I had ever been. If Hanuman failed to return before the first ray of the rising sun struck the earth, all would be lost. My body ached, my eyes blurred and still I did not doubt him.

All around me were the sounds of a dying army. Groans and signs and sobs rent the air. The monkey host had lost heart and with it, hope. The eastern rim of the earth looked paler. Any minute now . . . the sky above us darkened. 'Make way! Make way!' those of us still standing screamed. I could not believe my ailing eyes. A mountain was descending from the sky! Hanuman carried a mountain in his right hand! With a tremendous thud, he landed and placed the mountain in the middle of the battlefield.

'I was afraid to linger, looking for the herb that I may not have found,' he said to the physician. 'And so I uprooted the whole mountain and brought it!'

My weary heart soared. The physician was as amazed as the rest of us on the battlefield. But he had no time to waste. With deft hands, he found the Sanjivani herb and crushed the leaves to make a balm for Lakshman.

I looked at the horizon. Pale pink. The scent of the healing leaves filled the air. All around me, wounded warriors stirred to their feet, new vigour in their limbs. I sat up. The shafts fell out, painlessly. The first sunbeam burst free and Lakshman rose to his feet, strong and fit as ever. Rama embraced him, and Hanuman wept to see the two brothers reunited. And then Rama turned to him and embraced him too and Hanuman's face was flooded with joy.

Lakshman's recovery proved to be the turning point in the battle. Ravan was killed and the battle was won. The victorious monkey army escorted Rama, Lakshman and Sita home to their kingdom. Rama left Vibhishan behind to rule Lanka in Ravan's place, but he took Hanuman along. Rama's exile was over and he was installed as king. Everyone who helped him win the battle was royally rewarded. Hanuman alone sat quietly aside, not noticed, and seemingly forgotten. At last, when all the rewards had been given, Sita called him up to the throne and gave him a necklace studded with precious stones. Hanuman bowed deeply and took it. Some time later, the other courtiers noticed he was breaking open each stone, examining it closely and throwing it away. They found the sight hilarious.

'What are you looking for, O monkey-chief?' they asked mockingly. 'Something to *eat*, perhaps?'

'No,' said Hanuman solemnly. 'I am looking to see if these stones bear Rama's name.'

'Of course they do not!' they scoffed. 'They're precious stones, priceless gems, not peanuts to be cracked and thrown away like that!'

'In that case, they're worthless,' Hanuman said, sadly. 'For me the only thing that's precious is Rama's name.'

'What about your heart then?' they continued. 'Would that be useless if it didn't have Rama in it? Why don't you show us? Is Rama sitting there inside your heart?'

'Yes,' Hanuman answered, simply.

'Prove it!' the courtiers shouted, determined to humiliate the monkey-chief.

'All right,' said Hanuman, and without any warning he tore his chest open. The entire court gasped. Inside his chest, they saw Rama sitting with Sita and his brothers by his side. Rama rose from his throne. Hanuman swooned as his blood drained away. He was about to crumple and fall when Rama caught him, and embraced him. The touch of the lord whom he loved so much healed him and Hanuman became whole again.

'No one has been as faithful to me as you, Hanuman,' Rama said, holding him tightly. 'Not one of the courtiers here has shown me such love, such selflessness, such absolute devotion. You have risked your life, not once but again and again for me. You have flown thousands of miles bringing good news and healing herbs. You have never hesitated to put yourself in danger. For all of this I grant you a boon. Ask what you will.'

And Hanuman asked that he might live as long as Rama is remembered and so he lived forever, in stories of his valour and devotion, like this one.

In a flash, he **stretched out** his enormous body.

e were a great tribe. We lived in the forest by the river where the flowers were bright and the birds silly. You should have seen them fly, shrieking louder and louder as we approached, and then taking to the sky like tattered clouds. Though I myself was too respectable to take part in this game, I must say I fully understood the young monkeys' chattering glee each time this happened, which was very often. We ruled the upper treetops, you see. We swung, we looped, we leapt. We never wanted for food. Fruits hung ripe and ready in the trees of that generous jungle, juice dribbled, sap ran, sun shone. You could say that in that luxuriant forest, we were the tribe that luxuriated.

Our king was a king among monkeys. In our tribe, that's saying a lot. We have always had great warriors in our tribe, warriors whose faces are proud and feats are legend. In that sense, our king was a legend of legends. He was the strongest of our tribe, his fur shone like gold, his shoulders and arms were huge, and his agility was astounding. But it wasn't merely exceptional strength or an exceptional appearance that made him such a powerful king. No, it was his wisdom. Wisdom shone in his eyes like a light in the dark, and made us fear him, slightly. It was sharper than his tooth, and greater than his leap. They said he used his wisdom to understand the present and foretell the future. They said he knew things no monkey has ever known, and they were right. I worshipped him. He held us together and made us a great tribe.

One morning, we noticed our king was not himself. He sat, gravely, looking up the river. He sat for a long time. Then he called his band of trusty aides, which meant me and my men. We were the monkey's tails, to use an expression that is fast fading into disuse. Whatever he wanted done, we did for him. We arrived, and he said, 'How fast can you get your troops together?'

'At once!' I replied. War?

Our king continued, 'Take the troops to the mango grove upstream and have them pluck each and every fruit from each and every tree. Make sure not even one remains!'

Alas, not war. My aides, though excellent in their own way, are not too bright when it comes to something they've never done before. Plucking ripe and juicy mangoes, now there's something they couldn't be better at! But plucking them while still raw-green and sour— the thought boggled their monkey brains.

I must say even I was a bit unprepared for an order like that. 'What, Sire, could be the reason behind this mission?' I asked. 'Knowing the reason behind a mission increases motivation, Sire.'

I like to think of myself as some sort of military psychologist, you know troop morale and that sort of thing.

The king replied, gravely, 'Only one reason, to avoid disaster.'

It was clear that was all he was prepared to say. Who were we to argue?

We organized the troops and went swinging our merry way to

the mango grove, and then strip-strip the mangoes came, off every single tree. By the time the sun set, there wasn't a green mango in sight.

Pleased, as always, with my own efficiency, I reported back. 'It is done, Sire!' I announced. 'Not a single green mango remains hanging from a single tree!'

Our king nodded his head in acknowledgment. I must say I would have liked a little more appreciation. But who was I to argue. I retreated and we slept peacefully, as we did all nights.

. . .

The monkey tribe's peace would be short-lived. One solitary mango had escaped their sharp eyes and nimble hands. Hidden by a bird's nest, it turned golden-ripe in the sun, unseen, unnoticed. One day, heavy with juice, it fell off the branch into the flowing river. The swift current carried the golden mango downstream to where the king and his ministers were bathing. The king noticed it at once.

'What is that thing floating towards us?' he asked. 'Is it made of gold?'

'No Your Majesty,' said a quick-witted minister who had travelled much and seen many things. Quickly, he snatched the fruit out of the river and held it, glistening, in his hand. 'But it is certainly worth its weight in gold! This, Your Majesty, is a mango. A heavenly fruit, fit for kings. Indeed, in the lands where it grows abundantly, it is called the queen of all fruits.'

'Cut it and let me see if the people of those lands exaggerate,' the king said, for he was intrigued both by the minister's words and by the beauty of the unknown fruit. It was cut open. The juice ran thick and golden. The king ate a small piece, and was speechless. He ate another, then another.

'They do not exaggerate,' he said at last. 'It is priceless, this mango. Never have I tasted something so sweet, so juicy, so delicious! Find out at once where we can get more!'

'If it came floating down the river, Your Highness,' the quick-witted minister said, 'we can be sure that somewhere upstream, not far from here, is where the mango grove is.'

'Locate the grove and I will come and see it for myself,' the king ordered. The taste of this fruit had driven him mad for more.

. . .

We woke late that day. None of us were in a mood to be energetic. (Except of course the ever-perky young ones.) Normally by that time we would have scattered, some of us looking for food, some idly loitering, some scouting. But there we sat, all of us, yawning and scratching and soaking in the morning sun.

That's when we heard the faint sound of hooves.

Hooves? In our forest, that was unheard of. The young ones were chittering and yammering. We shushed them. A dread sound floated up to where we sat, hidden in the branches. Human voices!

'Here we are, Your Majesty,' said one. 'It's a magnificent mango grove, but there doesn't seem to be a single mango left. That's strange. I suggest we ride a bit further.'

The hooves sounded louder. They were galloping downstream from the grove to our camp. I threw a glance at our king. His face was majestic as always, but drawn. Like us, he was waiting.

'If I am not mistaken,' the same voice floated up. 'There must be marauders close by. To be precise . . .'

One of our young ones, who had been calmly eating a fruit, tossed the peel over his shoulder.

'Monkeys!'

It took them a second to locate us. There I was, staring directly into the slightly bulging eyes of a man. Row upon row of men looking straight at row upon row of monkeys. Us versus them.

'There!' said the one who stood beside the most grandly dressed, their king, I presumed. 'It is just as I suspected! Those monkeys have eaten every single one of the mangoes!'

'Unheard of!' their king bellowed. 'I am not letting these greedy brutes rob me of this divine fruit! That too from right under my nose! Get rid of the lot at once!'

'Now?' said another man. I realized dimness was not a trait restricted only to *my* aides.

'Well what do you think, next year?' their king barked. 'Right now! Shoot them all. I don't want a single one left alive!'

It came to me then why our king had ordered us to pluck all the raw fruit. He had hoped to avoid just such a scene. But one cursed fruit must have escaped us and it had drawn the men to our camp like honey draws bees. I threw a glance at our king, waiting for my orders. The men were already fitting arrows into their bows and picking up stones to fling at us.

'Quick!' our king said, his voice low but clear. 'Follow me!'

What? No troop formations? No battle-plan? Follow me? That was the kind of thing our young ones said when they played their little war-games. Wise though he was, and wonderful no doubt, I didn't think much of that order. We needed to re-group, find ammunition and fight back! We ruled the treetops, we were warriors and our feats were legendary. How would this 'follow-me' tactic go down in history? Badly. Very badly. At the slightest whiff of danger, the monkey tribe turns tail. My nostrils flared with annoyance. But who was I to argue?

Already the king had leapt ahead, already my trusty aides, trusty no longer it seems were leaping after him, already the she-monkeys grabbed their young ones and chattered angrily at those who wanted to stay. Already some of our best soldiers, broad of back and sturdy of limb, were pulling the aging ailing ones on to their shoulders, where they clung helpless as infants. It was a tide of fleeing monkey.

It swept past me as I stood, shocked and aggrieved, too stunned to join in. Some of the fiercer ones, bless their teeth and fur, were glaring and screaming at the men-soldiers below. The man-king was braver than mine. He led his soldiers to fight. Mine led his to flight. There we were shamefully running away, and there they were, pursuing us, clumsily yes, but pursuing. They stumbled over roots, they got caught in thickets and ran headlong into tree trunks. Their arrows misfired, and stuck quivering uselessly in wood. The sound of twanging, cursing, panting, galloping filled the steaming forest air.

What option did I have but to follow? I was the last to join that shameful surge, and I ran unwillingly, cursing, unheard, under my breath.

Never had our tribe travelled so far! This was unknown terrain. The trees changed, the creepers twisted in strange ways, we would have been lost if it hadn't been for our king, leaping on, undaunted, ahead of us. Even I knew that. Even in flight, he was kingly, curse him. He flew like the wind and we flew with him. It almost looked as if the ignominy of escape would be ours after all. The soldiers were tiring. Fewer arrows whistled past us than at the start. We were clear . . .

We were at the edge of a gorge. The forest ended abruptly, and where the next handhold should have been, there was merely air. Our king halted.

A yawning gap lay between the forest and the far side, where a bamboo grove stood. The gorge fell steep and endless. A leap across that gorge would be death. A thousand-foot fall to unseen rocks below. Screams. Death. My fur bristled, and not with anger. I had never come this close to death. Far worse than dying in battle would be this fall through thin air on to hard stone. Far worse. The gorge was impassable to both man and monkey. If it were up to me, I would turn now and fight, face them one on one, jump on to their necks and bite and scratch and die nobly. I would lead this battle, The Battle of Stony Gorge. I would be the last to flee, the first to fight! Glory would be mine, not cold and whistling death.

But not for me. Our king, wise and wonderful and mistaken, had other plans. In a flash he stretched out his enormous body, and grabbed a strong vine on the far side of the cliff. His feet still clung tightly to the tree that had been his perch.

'Hurry!' he said, in a voice that seemed to have grown as big as his body. 'Use me as a bridge. Climb over! At once!'

Escape, again. Howls of protest from my foolish aides. Trample on their king's majestic body to save their own worthless lives! It was unthinkable, it was . . . A tremendous roar cut short their feeble protests.

347

'Do as I say!' our king commanded.

And they did. Aghast, I watched our cowardice reach new depths. Trembling and asking forgiveness, they stepped on our king's enormous back and scampered across to the bamboo grove. Trembling and asking forgiveness, family after family clambered on and crossed. Hundreds and thousands of them. I alone stayed hidden and watched our king. I have always been blessed with prodigious sight. No hawk's eyes are keener than mine. I saw every detail. Our king's legendary strength was fading. His grip was beginning to weaken. His head was beginning to swim. He felt his arms and legs were being ripped off. He felt unable to endure for even one minute longer.

And still he did. I watched and I hated. I hated his grandeur, I hated his humility. How could he abase himself so for his people? How could he love so much, for so little? He was a disgrace to our tribe, the tribe of warrior monkeys. I hated his strength, I hated his gentleness. I had always done, but I had kept it cloaked under sweet words and worshipful manners. Now it all came out. I seethed as I watched. Great king, reduced to a lowly bridge of wood! All these years he had held himself aloof, apart, above us all in his power and his wisdom, now look at him! Dirt beneath our feet! How he had ignored me all these years, brushed aside my battle-plans, ignored my advice, ignored *me*! Well, now he would have to take notice.

The last of the tribe had crossed. It was my turn. I leapt on his back and stabbed him. I never travelled without my knife. No warrior would. And so with my warrior's knife, I stabbed our king and leapt across, laughing.

Our king would die, and I would watch.

. . .

The king had been watching the big monkey all this time. He had ridden along with his soldiers, thinking what a nice bit of sport it would be, but as they reached the gorge, it stopped being a sport.

'Hold your fire!' he ordered. 'Look at what is happening.'

The soldiers looked. The great big monkey, who must have been their leader, had turned himself into a bridge! At first they laughed and hooted, what brains, only a monkey would think of something so silly, but before long they were watching in silence.

The Monkey King's strength was failing. That was clear to see. He swayed, and his arms shook from the strain of holding on. There were too many monkeys. It was impossible. He would let go any minute now. He was going to fall . . . and yet he didn't. He hung on. The soldiers murmured admiringly. And then they gasped.

One monkey, lean and agile, had leapt across just when it seemed there was no one left, and what was this? He was stabbing the big monkey, repeatedly. Blood gushed out. The Monkey King shook all over. A traitor! The Monkey King let go of the vine, and in a last impossible act of will, drew himself back over that terrifying gorge, and lost his footing.

He tumbled off the tree that had been his perch and lay in a heap on the forest floor, exhausted and bleeding.

'Quick, help him revive!' the king ordered, getting off his horse. The soldiers lifted the dying monkey gently and placed his head on their king's lap.

The Monkey King's eyes fluttered open. He saw the king of the humans looking at him with wonder in his eyes.

'You astonish me, Monkey King,' the human king said, softly. 'Why did you do it? As one king to another, tell me. Why did you shed your own royal blood for them, who do not even deserve it?'

The Monkey King looked directly at his questioner with his old, infinitely wise eyes, and said, 'Because I am their king.' And then he gave a little gasp and died, right there in the other king's arms.

The human king found he had tears in his eyes. Looking up, he cried, 'This Monkey King is a better and braver king that I! Never before have I seen such strength, loyalty and devotion! From today I vow to be as worthy a king to my people as the Monkey King was to his. And from today, the monkey tribe is to be protected by us all, so that his sacrifice may not have been in vain!'

And so it was, that the Monkey King, who was none other than the Buddha himself, gave his life so that his people might live on, in peace.

AUTHOR'S NOTE

Adults sometimes act as if they know everything. The truth is, they don't. When I started writing this book, I had to do some serious brushing up on the things I *thought* I knew. First, I had to find the books I needed to read, and then . . . I had to read them. I had to look up websites that gave me the names of more websites. I had to make lists and counter-lists. I tore my hair out and wore my eyes out. It was, as you can imagine, absolute and utter fun. I discovered new things at every reading. I danced with glee each time I found how things matched. And then, when I had read and understood and found the stories that I wanted to tell, I closed the books, logged off the Internet and started to write. I do hope you have enjoyed what I wrote. If, when you're all 'growed' up, you feel like going on a trail of discovery like me, here's where you can start. These are the books I looked at, some in between covers like this one, some in the wide-open virtual space of the net. There could be no better way of finding the stories behind my stories. Happy reading on!

The Masks of God: Occidental Mythology by Joseph Campbell

Bundahis or The Original Creation (Translated by E.W. West)

Denkard (Translated by E. W. West, from *Sacred Books of the East,* Volume 5)

Denkard (Translated by Mary Boyce)

Vendidad (Translated by James Darmesteter)

Muhammad: A Biography of the Prophet by Karen Armstrong

'Adam: A Mohammedan Legend' (From *Biblical Legends of the Mussulmans*) by Dr G. Weil

Classical Hindu Mythology: A Reader in the Sanskrit Puranas (Edited and translated by Cornelia Dimmitt and J.A.B. van Buitenen)

The Vedic Experience—The Deluge Samplava 17 SB I, 8, 1, 1–10 (Translated by Professor Raimon Panikkar)

The Mahabharata (Translated by Kisari Mohan Ganguli)

Ramayan of Valmiki (Translated by Ralph T.H. Griffith)

The Bible—King James Version (Authorized): Genesis, Exodus, 1 Samuel, Daniel, The Gospel According to St. Matthew, The Gospel According to St. Mark, The Gospel According to St. Luke, The Gospel According to St. John

Catholic Encyclopaedia <http://www.newadvent.org>

Buddha, The Gospel by Paul Carus

'Nidana-katha: The Story of the Lineage' (Translated by T.W. Rhys Davids, from *Buddhist Birth Stories*)

'Buddhanusmrti: The Life of Gautama Buddha' <http://ccbs.ntu.edu.tw/DBLM/resource/ebooks>

Saddharma-Pundarika Sutra (Translated by H. Kern)

Jataka Tales

The Kalpasutra of Bhadrabahu: The Life of Mahavira (Translated by Hermann Jacobi)

Akaranga Sutra (Translated by Hermann Jacobi)

Life of Guru Nanak: The Sikh Religion, Volume 1 by Max Arthur MacAuliffe

<http://www.ikonkar.com/sikhism/>

And above all, one invaluable site:
<http://www.sacred-texts.com>

ABOUT THE AUTHOR

Born in Africa, Sampurna Chattarji started her writing career as a copywriter with J. Walter Thompson, India. An award-winning poet and short-story writer, she has also spent time as creative director of a Singapore-based website and inventor of her own brand of nonsense. Her translation of Sukumar Ray's poetry and prose titled *Abol Tabol: The Nonsense World of Sukumar Ray* has been published by Puffin.

Sampurna lives in Mumbai.